"[Stan Toler's] writings do not come from a journalism classroom, but rather out of day to day experiences. His style is unique in that it does not take him long until he has you walking along side him as he kicks the cans down a lonely West Virginia road, or cry[ing] with him and his brother outside the hospital in North Columbus, holding Linda's hand with him as he prays for the love of his life, or cheering for a son at the stadium. He takes you with him in his every day walk.

You will not read Stan long until you know the real man. A man of sterling character, full of God, and filled with a love for everyone he meets. I have never read any of his books without being able to say 'I read Toler today for my daily faith lift.'"

—Dr. Alton Loveless
President/CEO of Randall House Publications

"I have read all of the books by Stan Toler (and we wrote four together). But this is his best book ever, and funniest. You will love reading it because of all the humorous illustrations, but you will learn from reading it because of the many principles drawn from Bible references. Also, you will live better because of the multitude of practical observations, and finally you will become more holy because the book will draw you closer to God.

In this occasion Stan Toler has communicated Christian principles with humor, contemporary illustrations, and a writing style that reflects the *USA Today,* i.e., it is crisp, contemporary, and compelling."

—Elmer L. Towns
Dean, School of Religion, Liberty University

"*The Buzzards are Circlin' But God's not Finished with Me Yet* has enough humor to keep you entertained, enough stories and examples to keep you interested, enough Scripture to keep you grateful for God's grace and goodness, and enough practical advice to make it a good investment of your time and money."

—Zig Ziglar
Author and Motivational Teacher,
Dallas, Texas

"With his typical warmth, wit, and wisdom, Stan Toler has written a book that will help you through the difficult days of your life. *The Buzzards are Circling, but God's Not Finished with Me Yet* is a book for these times. You cannot read it without being reminded of God's constant love and care in the midst of a crisis."

—Norman G. Wilson
General Director of Communications,
The Wesleyan Church

The Buzzards Are Circling, but God's Not Finished with Me Yet

The Buzzards Are Circling, but God's Not Finished with Me Yet

by

Stan Toler

HONOR **HB** BOOKS

FROM DAVID C. COOK

THE BUZZARDS ARE CIRCLING, BUT GOD'S NOT FINISHED WITH ME YET
Published by Honor Books®, an imprint of
David C. Cook
4050 Lee Vance View
Colorado Springs, CO 80918 U.S.A.

David C. Cook Distribution Canada
55 Woodslee Avenue, Paris, Ontario, Canada N3L 3E5

David C. Cook U.K., Kingsway Communications
Eastbourne, East Sussex BN23 6NT, England

David C. Cook and the graphic circle C logo
are registered trademarks of Cook Communications Ministries.

Unless otherwise indicated, all Scripture quotations are taken from the *Holy Bible, New International Version®. NIV®.* Copyright © 1973, 1978, 1984 by International Bible Society. Used by permission of Zondervan Publishing House. All rights reserved. Scripture quotations marked KJV are taken from the King James Version of the Bible. Public Domain.

ISBN 978-1-58919-305-5

© 2001 by STAN TOLER
Printed in the United States of America
First Edition 2001

15 16 17 18 19 20 21

090907

Dedication

In memory of my lovely mother-in-law

Nadine Carter

1925-2000

Special Thanks

—Mark Gilroy, Shawna McMurry, Jeff Dunn, Debbie Justus, and the RiverOak Publishing team. Thanks for your confidence in me.

—Jerry Brecheisen for editorial guidance, research, creative insights, and Christian brotherhood.

—Mark Toler-Hollingsworth, Terry Toler, and Debra White Smith for ideas, encouragement, and laughter.

—Pat Diamond for proofreading; and Deloris Leonard for typing, editing, proofreading, and daily support in my office.

Table of Contents

Foreword

Stan Toler is undoubtedly one of the most gifted and brilliant people I know.

When he tells about wrecking his car in his own driveway, I figure not just anybody could do that. Such a feat definitely takes talent and plenty of brains! I know! I recently had a fender bender at my own curb. My housekeeper made the fatal mistake of parking her car in front of my house, too close to my driveway, and at the exact angle where my "boat" van could mesh with her bumper. While the poor woman was inside blissfully cleaning my home, I smashed her bumper. I went inside and informed her of my brilliant undertaking. After about fifteen minutes of head scratching and analyzing, the two of us figured out how to disconnect our vehicles. My housekeeper wound up having to file on my insurance to have her bumper fixed. Looks like Stan isn't the only one who's got the level of talent needed to have a wreck at two miles an hour!

I was just as blessed to read about Stan's faux pas in preaching. He claims that any time he says "without a doubt" behind the pulpit, his two brothers understand that means he knows nothing about what he is saying. Stan recounts the time when he was preaching at the ripe old age of seventeen, and he said, "Without a doubt, the Ethiopian eunuch was a good provider for his wife and children." Of course, I screamed with laughter for several minutes when I read that one. Part of my laughter was from outright hilarity, and part of it was from relief. I'm thrilled to know that other speakers have made as many goofy mistakes as I have while standing behind the microphone. Like the time I said, "If you're looking for the Old Testament in Greek, you won't find it." Oh, duh! Then there was the time I sprang forth with, "There's a cliché, beauty from ashes." That one is a double duh! Especially when you read Isaiah 61:3 KJV, *"To appoint unto them that mourn in Zion, to give unto them beauty for ashes, the oil of joy for mourning, the garment of praise for the spirit of heaviness; that they might be called trees of righteousness, the planting of the LORD, that he might be glorified."*

While Stan details numerous hilarious stories to which many of us can relate, he also addresses the buzzards that are inevitable in everyone's life. For instance, that unexpected phone call about a fatal wreck—not just a fender bender in the driveway; bankruptcy; the grim line of a doctor's mouth when he says "inoperable"; getting fired; loss of faith in a compromising spiritual leader; divorce; a child who goes to prison—and deserves it.

No matter what form the buzzards take, the pain is universal. As I travel across the U.S. and speak, I repeatedly meet devout saints who have seen the buzzards circlin', or perhaps they've tasted the ashes and are straining to find the beauty.

As Stan would so eloquently say, "without a doubt," we all have adversities. Or perhaps, "I'm certain that life is full of uncertainties" as well, "but I could be wrong about that." Yet one thing stands true. Jesus loves me. He loves you. And He will strengthen you to withstand the attacks of any buzzards that might try to devour your life. God really isn't finished with you, despite the circlin' buzzards. He really will give you beauty for ashes, joy for mourning, and praise for the spirit of heaviness. He really will glorify His name in your life. And Stan Toler will encourage you to stand and embrace life anew with the zest of one who has survived the storms, come through with a firmer faith in Jesus Christ, and pledged to break forth with joy. As Stan so beautifully underscores, no buzzard can prevail in the face of Christ's victory; no ashes can remain in the wake of God's joy. Divine victory is yours to embrace. Embrace it, and find a power for living you have never known before.

—Debra White Smith

Introduction

As I write this, a flock of buzzards is flying in formation over the Toler household.

My mother-in-law passed away.

My father-in-law is in the hospital.

My stepfather is in the hospital.

I just wrecked my new car (in my own driveway while I was trying to pick up the newspaper). Like a nearsighted driver's ed student, I nailed the brick wall by the house and took all the light potential out of our yard lantern!

Besides that, when I arrived at the office the other day, I discovered that the faithful custodian at my church had mopped the tile floor in the foyer—and didn't tell me! I took a vigorous step onto the tile and immediately took flight, one hand outstretched (my briefcase was flapping in my other hand). Now I've got bruises in places that haven't even been declared "bruisable" by the government!

Some of you are bruised as well. Life, at its worst, took a swing at you while you weren't looking. And now the buzzards are circlin' overhead. If so, you're the reason I put these words on paper.

17

Have you ever seen buzzards fly south for the winter? Neither have I. It's my understanding that they are migratory birds, but I'm at a loss to know whether they head south to Miami, west to Capistrano, or pack their onboard luggage for some other sunny climate.

I can just imagine them flying along in a *V* formation until one of them spots lunch. Suddenly the hungry bird banks right and immediately ruins the configuration. The ravenous culprit wrecks the air show with no sense of remorse. His fellow buzzards aren't too critical though. They know that their fellow "snowbird" is only doing what buzzards normally do: feeding off the infirmities of others.

I have seen undertakers fly south for the winter, however. Some of them are my dear friends, and I've ridden in the coach section of an airplane with one or two. I don't want to offend either buzzards or undertakers. But I'll go on record as saying that undertakers have one thing in common with buzzards: sharing the title of the last chapter of this book. (And, I must admit, the fact that I am spending the remaining days of my life trying to evade the mission of both groups!)

This is a sequel to my book *God Has Never Failed Me, but He's Sure Scared Me to Death a Few Times.* In that book, I refer to the List, "You Know It's Going to Be a Bad Day When. . . ." One indication that you're going to have a bad day: "The bird singing outside your bedroom window is a buzzard."[1]

Let's face it, there are times when we are weakened by our circumstances. There are times when it seems to be "Us vs. Life," and Life is up by three points with less than two minutes to go in the last quarter. This is a playbook for the two-minute warnings of our lives. It's during those two-minute-warning situations when the buzzards rev up their engines for a flight over our circumstances.

This book isn't filled with all the answers. No earthly author has all the answers (no matter what it says on the dust jacket of their book). It is filled with God's answers though, answers that are as relevant as the sunrise—and just as dependable.

God has spoken to the circumstances of our lives—buzzards circlin' or otherwise. He doesn't send us into voice mail when we cry out to Him in pain, confusion, or grief. By the inspiration of the Holy Spirit, He instructed forty-some writers to express His concern and His promises of deliverance in the book of all books, the Bible.

In the next pages, you will experience a light look at some pretty heavy subjects:

World-crumbling situations

Letting God take control

Testing times—building times

Learning to cope

Finding a purpose in the pain

and more . . .

I pray that these pages will be informative as well as inspirational, thought provoking as well as funny, motivational as well as spiritual. But most of all, I pray that they will be faithful to the Word of God. It is the only book that has truly helped me face times of joy, grief, pain, adversity, or advancement in my own life.

And I hope that when the buzzards start circling over the two-minute-warning times in your life, this book will be a reminder that God isn't finished with you yet.

You are loved,
Stan Toler

When Your World Crumbles, You Don't Have to Be One of the Crumbs

(You Can Survive Your Situation)

David Hopkins felt as if the eyes of a thousand demons penetrated his soul as he walked across the campus of Emanuel College in Franklin Springs, Georgia. Thousands of beady-eyed buzzards arrogantly shifted along the bare tree limbs as if they were waiting for him to drop dead and furnish them lunch. My friend Dr. Hopkins, the college president, said his skin crawled as he thought about the six years of torture that had come from the predators who had arrived regularly in October and lingered until April, infesting the college property.

With the crunch of his every footstep on the leaf-strewn ground, he relived the staff's repeated efforts to scare away the birds. Devoted employees tried banging pots and pans—and even firing warning shots into the air. Nothing worked. And killing the ebony beasts was against the law. According to local officials, the tormentors were endangered. Destroying them would result in a hefty fine. The cold autumn wind tearing at the trees seemed to mock Dr. Hopkins, and he was certain one swooping buzzard grinned with glee!

Indeed, the buzzards seemed a metaphor for the spiritual warfare of the last six years. As the winged menaces invaded the school, year in and year out, David's wife almost died of cancer. He suffered from the sometimes fatal Crohn's disease. The college, in the throes of necessary but difficult change, struggled for financial survival. Dr. Hopkins wondered if and when the buzzards would smell the death of the college and swoop. He shook his fist toward the feathered foes and declared, "You won't win!"

Yet just when it looked like he was finished, twenty-five prayer warriors arrived on the campus to pray for the college—and for the rapid departure of the carnivorous creatures. The next day, Dr. Hopkins received a call from a donor who said, "I'll give $160,000 toward the construction of the new science building." Another donor called and said, "We'll give $500,000 toward the new science building!" What's more, his wife was declared cancer free!

President Hopkins told me that he was so happy about the news that he nearly "floated home." That's when he made a startling discovery. As he looked around, he noticed the trees were void of those dark adversaries. No buzzards! Gone! Gone! Gone! For no apparent reason, they had vanished! At that moment, he recalled Abraham's sojourn from Ur to the Promised Land. Abraham had paused to worship and to offer a sacrifice to God as a symbol of his covenant to be obedient, regardless of circumstances! (It should be noted: The buzzards came down to steal Abraham's sacrifice before he could seal it. Abraham had to *shoo* the winged predators away!)

Someday, you're going to spot buzzards circling in your spiritual "No-Fly Zone." There is going to come a time when you're hit with a crisis, one that you didn't see coming. And it may cause your whole world to crumble like an old cookie that's met with a big sledgehammer. But take heart; you don't have to be a *crumb* in the midst of the crumbling.

WORLD CRUMBLING IS NOT AN OLYMPIC SPORT

The Old Testament character Job reminds us: *"Man is born to trouble as surely as sparks fly upward"* (Job 5:7). It's a fact of life. We didn't inherit curly hair, brown eyes, and a propensity to arthritis from Adam. We inherited trouble. Adam's disobedience to God started a chain reaction of suffering and sorrow that won't be broken until the eastern sky splits and the Savior returns. The Bible says, *"In Adam all die."* (1 Corinthians 15:22).

So our family tree is more like a prickly cactus than a pristine maple. But how does it play out in the landscape of life? There are several factors that can play a part in those world-crumbling times.

LIFE CHANGES

We are spiritually and emotionally vulnerable when we face changes in the routine of our lives. Vocational, housing, relationship, physical, or financial changes—all may reduce our *stability* to zero, to put a new slant on the fog report! In the Old Testament, Abraham faced unsettling uncertainty when God called him to leave his homeland and take his family to a new country.

He responded obediently, but I'm sure there was a king-size knot in his stomach when he packed his luggage. *"By faith Abraham, when called to go to a place he would later receive as his inheritance, obeyed and went, even though he did not know where he was going"* (Hebrews 11:8). "Not knowing where he was going" is key to what he must have felt. Everything familiar would soon be set aside, and he would leap like a sky diver into the unknown.

The focus is on Abraham because of the patriarchal emphasis in Bible times. But think about how his family must have felt. They would have to leave those familiar department stores and playgrounds, forfeit soccer-team membership, subscribe to a new cable television service.

Sad farewells.

Financial uncertainty.

Strange roads.

This wasn't going to be a picnic for Abraham's family.

Change never is a picnic, but it happens. When it does, our world often crumbles. Sudden layoffs. Diving stocks. Rising gas prices. A doctor with a somber face, holding an alarming medical report in his hands.

> *Happiness is inward and not outward; and so it does not depend on what we have, but on what we are.*
> —*Henry Van Dyke*

What is it that makes our world come tumbling down like a planetary Humpty-Dumpty? There are several causes.

DELAYED PROMISES

Look again at Abraham's life story: *"By faith he made his home in the promised land like a stranger in a foreign country; he*

lived in tents, as did Isaac and Jacob, who were heirs with him of the same promise. For he was looking forward to the city with foundations, whose architect and builder is God" (Hebrews 11:9-10).

Abraham was looking forward to the city.

So, where's the city? All he saw was desert. No skyscrapers here, just dusty tent dwellings at the end of long travel days spent looking at the backside of a camel.

This was supposed to be the Promised Land. But for Abraham, it must have looked like it was mostly *land* and little *promise*. For the moment, milk and honey looked more like curds and why?

Delayed promises are world-crumbling situations. We gather together the hopes and pledges of the Bible like a pile of prescriptions from an immediate-care clinic. We haul out our inheritance claims. We thumb through the Rolodex of advice from near and far. "Just a little while." "Sunday's coming." "Somewhere over the rainbow. . . ."

But we're used to instant coffee and microwave popcorn. Delayed promises? We've been promised a celestial city, but we can't see it for the storm clouds. The realization sets in and causes our hearts to break. We're stuck in the now, like Abraham and his family, trying to eke out an existence in an unfurnished Promised-Land apartment.

PERSONAL PROBLEMS

Abraham also had to look for a promise beyond the horizon of personal setbacks. *"By faith Abraham, even though he*

27

was past age—and Sarah herself was barren—was enabled to become a father because he considered him faithful who had made the promise. And so from this one man, and he as good as dead, came descendants as numerous as the stars in the sky and as countless as the sand on the seashore" (Hebrews 11:11-12).

Wouldn't it be awful to face life when you've already been declared "as good as dead"? Maybe you have!

The buzzards of age and infirmity had been in a holding pattern over Abraham's life. God had made the promise: Abraham's descendants would be as numerous as the stars. But Abraham couldn't see the stars because of the smudges on his trifocals. His family would become as numerous as the sands, but the sands of his own hourglass had settled quicker than an elephant in a lawn chair.

We've all been there. Personal difficulties crowd out our hopes of a tomorrow. We can't do *that* because of *this*. "If only I could. . . ." "I just wish I didn't have to. . . ." "If it weren't for. . . ." We dialogue with life, wishing we could erase the effects of time. Personal difficulties swarm around us:

Grudges that poison us

Jealousy that gnaws at us

Loneliness that isolates us

Inadequacies that paralyze us

Finances that bind us

Sorrows that plague us.

SUDDEN TRIALS

Abraham's life would have been so much different if it weren't for *that day*. He had been sailing along—working out the issues of a new home, bringing his family to a consensus, driving fresh-cut stakes into the promises of the new land. Then, the Scriptures say, *"God tested Abraham"* (Genesis 22:1). Abraham had *that day!*

A sudden trial arrived like a five-hundred-pound gorilla. God was applying a litmus test to Abraham. He wanted His protégé to see that faith works when we face *that day*. God told Abraham to take his son to a remote place and prepare an altar of sacrifice—and then to sacrifice his son, his only son, back to God. Leaving his servants behind, Abraham took the materials for the altar, along with his only son, and began the longest journey of his life. The trip from Ur was a piece of cake compared to these few steps.

Even as they walked together, the questions began to fly: "Father, where's the sacrifice?" Abraham's heart was pounding. He was committed to obey God's command: to make his own son that sacrifice. Abraham replied, "God will provide." But deep in his heart the doubts must have swirled like an oak leaf in a whirlpool.

That day—that sudden testing time in the life of the patriarch that would be unlike any other day. *"By faith Abraham, when God tested him, offered Isaac as a sacrifice. He who had received the promises was about to sacrifice his one and only son"* (Hebrews 11:17). Abraham passed the test. He trusted God beyond what common sense or his own will would have led him to do. Then God instructed Abraham not to lay a hand on his son and provided a ram for Abraham to sacrifice.

Perhaps you've had a day like that. Life was pretty uneventful, then suddenly everything changed. A sound of metal crushing metal. A telephone call. A knock on the door. An ambulance siren. We who are children of promise suddenly face a horrendous situation. Something is expected of us. Not one of us is exempt.

I'M HAVING A "WHOLE LIFE" CRISIS

Our reactions to world-crumbling events vary.

Sometimes we feel helpless. For the most part, we're used to being in control of things. But when life is suddenly out of control, a sense of vulnerability sets in. Until now, we've been able to fix most everything else, but we can't fix this. It's just out of reach, like that burned-out lightbulb in the twenty-foot ceiling chandelier. We can see it, and we know that changing it would make a difference. But without some assistance, we're powerless.

Sometimes we feel abandoned. Alone in the hospital room, waiting for loved ones. Alone at the table that once was also occupied by a spouse or parent. Alone in a courtroom hallway, waiting for the lawyer. Alone. Abandoned. "Why me, Lord?" we inquire. But often, Heaven is silent—not because there isn't any concern up there, but because we make such loud groaning noises down here that we cannot hear the still, small voice of assurance.

Character cannot be developed in ease and quiet. Only through experience of trial and suffering can the soul be strengthened, vision cleared, ambition inspired, and success achieved.
—*Helen Keller*

Sometimes we feel worthless. World-crumbling events have a way of sucking the self-esteem out of our lives. Our pride and dignity are temporarily gone. Our once-secure finances are tenuous. Our once-strong bodies are frail. Our once-happy homes are in shambles. Our once-respectful children have rebelled. We feel about as significant as an eyelash on a mosquito.

Sometimes we feel ashamed. Sometimes we have made a personal contribution to the world-crumbling situation. We've been players, not just bystanders. Sometimes we make wrong choices. We cross the line. The pain in the foot comes from a self-inflicted gunshot wound. We stand in our self-made ruins and weep over what should have been, or what might have been, if only we had kept the law of God or if only we had let our conscience give the final answer.

One day, Jesus came across a man who was a poster child for world-crumbling events:

> *Jesus went up to Jerusalem for a feast of the Jews. Now there is in Jerusalem near the Sheep Gate a pool, which in Aramaic is called Bethesda and which is surrounded by five covered colonnades. Here a great number of disabled people used to lie—the blind, the lame, the paralyzed.*
>
> *One who was there had been an invalid for thirty-eight years. When Jesus saw him lying there and learned*

that he had been in this condition for a long time, he
asked him, "Do you want to get well?"

"Sir," the invalid replied, "I have no one to help me
into the pool when the water is stirred. While I am try-
ing to get in, someone else goes down ahead of me."

Then Jesus said to him, "Get up! Pick up your mat
and walk." At once the man was cured; he picked up his
mat and walked.

John 5:1-9

For thirty-eight years of his life, this man had been carried, pulled, or pushed to the pool beside the sheep gate on the northern side of the Jerusalem temple. There the unnamed man, with so many unnamed others, waited to be healed.

The invalids believed that an angel of the Lord occasionally stirred the waters in the pool and the first person to step into the water would be healed.

This poor man had never made it. Though he had helpers to transport him and put him close to the edge of the pool, he had never been *first in*. This day was no exception. It was "miracle time," and he was tardy.

Time after time, he was toenail close to a miracle. But still, he went to the pool!

Think of the cruelty. A heavenly messenger makes a house call every now and then but brings only enough healing power to cure just one person: the first one in.

Jesus saw and approached this man. He learned about the man's plight, and the Lord healed him. And the fact is, when our world crumbles, Jesus never fails to see it, and He is never far away.

God believes in me,
Therefore my situation is never hopeless.
God walks with me,
Therefore I am never alone.
God is on my side,
Therefore I can never lose.
—Anonymous

Life Is Full of Uncertainty . . . but I Could Be Wrong about That

(Gaining Confidence in Tough Times)

Early in my ministry, I often preached beyond my knowledge of the Scriptures. Pastoring my first church when I was only seventeen years of age, I was forced to put together some homiletic gems. To appear that I knew my subject well, I would confidently use the phrase, "without a doubt." My preacher brothers, Mark and Terry, have this saying: "When Stan uses the phrase, 'without a doubt,' he doesn't have a clue what he's talking about."

Life is full of uncertainties. Of that, I can say, "Without a doubt." I've lived long enough to know that nothing is a sure thing. Ira Stanphill penned these words about life's uncertainties:

> *Many things about tomorrow*
> *I don't seem to understand;*
> *But I know who holds tomorrow,*
> *And I know who holds my hand.*[2]

God's hand is outstretched to you today. Reach out, take His strong hand, and let Him guide you through the unsettling times of your life.

In uncertain times, I recommend these steps:

1. Quit feeling sorry for yourself!

In "The Jonah Syndrome," Eugene Peterson says, "Pity is one of the noblest emotions available to human beings; self-pity is possibly the most ignoble. Pity is the capacity to enter into the pain of another in order to do something about it; self-pity is an incapacity, a crippling emotional disease that severely distorts our perception of reality. Pity discovers the need in others for love and healing and then fashions speech and action that bring strength; self-pity reduces the universe to a personal wound that is displayed as proof of significance. Pity is adrenaline for acts of mercy; self-pity is a narcotic that leaves its addicts wasted, a derelict."[3]

There is nothing as pitiful as a pity party. I know because I have been asked to supply the refreshments for several! As a pastor, I have been asked, on many occasions, to attend pity parties. Usually, I haven't received formal invitations. Many of them were not that well planned. And some were even quite spontaneous.

The atmosphere of a pity party has never been that attractive to me. Grim face masks, floor-level countenance, wet eyes—it's not a party you would want to bring a guest to. And what intrigues me most is that there is no music. What's a party without music? Nobody sings at a pity party. There's no accordion. There's no dancing (especially if you're a Nazarene preacher like me!).

And the saddest of all: pity parties sap all the energy from those who throw them. There is nothing left. Some of that energy could have been used to help another who had suffered a world-crumbling situation!

Before she became a Christian, the late Ethel Waters, a performer who often sang at Billy Graham crusades, was best known for her rendition of the popular song "Stormy

Weather." Later, after she had become a Christian, she was asked to sing the song. She replied, "No, sir, I'll never sing 'Stormy Weather' again. Since Jesus came into my heart, I've never had stormy weather like I had before I knew Him."

2. Be honest with yourself.

So often we camouflage our worries and fears from others, and in the process we fool ourselves. Romans 12:3 says, *"Do not think of yourself more highly than you ought, but rather think of yourself with sober judgment, in accordance with the measure of faith God has given you."* That includes the good, bad, and the ugly.

Being honest with yourself is a difficult task. It's much easier to create an illusion or to fake it—or simply to quit or to give up. Don't even think about throwing in the towel, for God is not finished with you yet. You're not perfect; you are human—made from the dust of the earth. Be realistic about your strengths and honest about your weaknesses.

Honesty and humility go together.

I like the story of the newly elected congressman who thought a little more highly of himself than he should have. He went to his new office on Capitol Hill. The only things in his office were a chair, a desk, and a telephone.

He sat down in his big, burgundy leather executive chair. Into his office came a man who appeared to be a news reporter. The freshman congressman thought he'd better pick up the phone and act important. So he carried on the following fictitious conversation, "Yes, Mr. President, I'm doing well—the office is great! How's the family? No, I'm sorry, I can't make it for dinner tonight—I'm working on a very important piece of legislation. Perhaps another time. Best to you, too, sir!"

He hung up the phone and said, "So, are you with MSNBC? CNN?"

The man replied, "No, I'm with AT&T, and I'm here to hook up your phone."

3. Change your outlook.

It's a classic theory: Attitude affects your altitude. We will never see a sunrise on the mountaintop if we choose to set up a mental campsite in the valley. World-crumbling events may change everything around us, but they don't have to change us. We can rise above them—inside, where it really counts.

Charles Swindoll said, "The longer I live, the more I realize the impact of attitude on life. Attitude, to me, is more important than facts. It is more important than the past, than education, than money, than circumstances, than failures, than successes, than what other people think or say or do. It is more important than appearance, giftedness, or skill. It will make or break a company . . . a church . . . a home. The remarkable thing is we have a choice every day regarding the attitude we will embrace for that day. We cannot change our past. . . . We cannot change the fact that people will act in a certain way. We cannot change the inevitable. The only thing we can do is play on the one string we have, and that is our attitude. . . . I am convinced that life is 10 percent what happens to me and 90 percent how I react to it. . . . We are in charge of our attitudes."[4]

The Worst "Bad Word" in the World

Try to think of all the words
That you could live without;
Make a list of all those words
And throw the worst word out.
It's not a very easy task,
You might just rave and rant;
But don't give up before you find
The worst bad word is "Can't."

—*Charles Chigna*

4. Grow your gratitude.

If you're reading this, the chances are you're still alive! Aren't you thankful for that? Gratitude takes our attention off the misery and puts it on the mercy. The New Testament apostle Paul gave us some pretty good advice, *"Give thanks in all circumstances, for this is God's will for you in Christ Jesus"* (1 Thessalonians 5:18). Some folks spend half of their fortunes and most of their lives wondering and worrying about what God wants them to do. The bottom line is, God's will doesn't begin on some mission field on the far corner of Survivor Island. It begins at home—in our hearts—by our being thankful for what He has already done.

When we take time to reflect on the miracles of life—health, home, family, and all the rest—it gives us a better perspective on the areas we consider problem areas. And, of course, the greatest consideration should be given for God's provision of acceptance and forgiveness, a provision made possible through the Lord Jesus Christ.

A young girl carried her beginner's book and slowly approached the grand piano, left center of the platform. Kim Hawk was all of ten years old—a child with Down's syndrome.

More than a thousand worshipers silently cheered for her as she opened the book and began to play the Sunday morning offertory. With one finger, Kim painstakingly pecked out "Jesus Loves Me." At times she paused indefinitely, struggling to place her stubby, little fingers on the right keys. Her brow wrinkled in concentration; her lips puckered with determination; her eyes narrowed with intensity.

As Kim continued in her simple, pure worship, my own heart swelled with God's love—perfect, holy, blameless. "Yes, Jesus loves me. / Yes, Jesus loves me. / Yes, Jesus loves me. / The Bible tells me so."

At last, Kim finished and slipped off the piano bench. An avalanche of applause punctuated her message. "Jesus loves me!" swelled from every heart as God's Spirit filled that sanctuary with the force of His infinite power. Grown men, breathing deeply, struggled to retain their dignity while weepy women searched for tissues to blot their damp cheeks.

Without any doubt, Kim Hawk has more friends than anyone I know. She doesn't grumble about not being able to play as easily as someone else. Instead, she joyfully uses what God has given her to give praise to Him and share His love with others.

> *Count your blessings instead of crosses;*
> *Count your gain instead of losses.*
> *Count your joys instead of woes;*
> *Count your friends instead of foes.*
> *Count your smiles instead of tears;*
> *Count your courage instead of fears.*
> *Count your full years instead of lean;*
> *Count your kind deeds instead of mean.*
> *Count your health instead of wealth;*
> *Count on God instead of yourself!*
> *—Anonymous*

5. Determine to be happy.

In the hills of West Virginia, we often sang in children's church, "If you're happy and you know it, say, 'Amen!'" That song is easy to sing when you are a child. As a teenager, I often sang, "Don't worry, be happy." But I learned quickly that "happy" doesn't come naturally. In fact, one of our first acts on earth was to cry and complain! Happiness is a choice, an act of the will. H.L. Mencken once said, "A cynic is a man who, when he smells flowers, looks around for a coffin." What we think is even more important than what happens to us. We have a decision to make when we encounter world-crumbling situations. They will either rob us of our joy, or they will enhance it.

Actually, adversity is the soil where victory is grown.

There's even a physiological advantage to positive thinking in problem situations. Research indicates that it takes seventy hours to physically overcome just one negative thought. It also takes twenty-one days to replace a habit or negative way of thinking. And we should also be warned that negative thinking may shorten our life span by sixteen years.

Did you know that you have the opportunity to face life just like a frog in a can of cream? If not, then read on:

Two frogs fell into a can of cream,
   Or so I've heard it told.

The sides of the can were shiny and steep,
   The cream was deep and cold.

"Oh, what's the use?" said Number One,
   'Tis fate, no help's around.

Good-bye, my friend! Good-bye, sad world!"
   And weeping still, he drowned.

But Number Two, of sterner stuff,
   Dog paddled in surprise.

The while he wiped his creamy face,
   And dried his creamy eyes,

"I'll swim awhile, at least," he said,
   Or so it has been said,

"It really wouldn't help the world
   If one more frog was dead."

An hour or two he kicked and swam,
   Not once he stopped to mutter,

But kicked and swam, and swam and kicked,
   Then hopped out, via butter.

                                    —Anonymous

6. Ask God for help.

For some, the last person they go to in times of plenty is the first person they seek in times of problems. "God, help me!" seems to be the reoccurring prayer at the scene of a problem. And rightly so! The Psalmist said, *"God is our refuge and strength, an ever-present help in trouble"* (Psalm 46:1).

A little boy answered the phone. "Hello."

A voice on the other end asked for his mother.

The boy replied, "She can't come to the phone. She's outside talking to the policeman."

The caller said, "Okay, then let me speak to your dad."

The boy replied, "Sorry. He's outside talking to the policeman.

Curious, the caller asked, "Why is everybody outside talking to the policeman?"

The boy responded in a hushed voice, "They're all looking for me."

We don't have to go looking for God when the storms come. He's already there. There isn't a single drop of rain that is unfamiliar to Him. The winds and the waves are His humble servants. And the clouds of time will transport His glorious Son from the heavens to usher us into the realms of eternity.

We can be assured that if our world crumbles, He is able to repair it. After all, He holds the patent on it!

An anonymous writer penned these insightful words:

> *So together we stand at life's crossroads*
> *And view what we think is the end,*

But God has a much bigger vision
And He tells us it's only a bend.

For the road goes on and is smoother,
And the pause in the song is a rest.
And the part that's unsung and unfinished
Is the sweetest and richest and best.

So rest and relax and grow stronger.
Let go and let God share your load,
Your work is not finished or ended,
You've just come to a bend in the road.

GOOD NEWS/BAD NEWS IS MOSTLY GOOD

Life is full of good news/bad news situations. An old friend of mine, David Felter, recently told me, "In 1991, the average person faced seven adverse situations a day. Today, they face twenty-three." Come to think of it, he never got around to telling me the good news!

I will settle for this old story about two baseball fanatics to illustrate my point. They had agreed that whoever died first would try to come back and tell the other if there was baseball in Heaven.

A few months later, one died during the seventh-inning stretch at a major-league baseball game. And a year later, the remaining fan heard a strange voice in his sleep, "Joe! Joe!"

Joe was startled and awoke. "Fred, is that you?"

"Yes," his buddy responded. "I've got some good news and some bad news."

"No kidding! Give me the good news first," he replied.

Fred answered, "Well, the good news is that there *is* baseball up here!"

Joe asked, "And the bad?"

Fred responded, "The bad news is, you're scheduled to pitch tomorrow afternoon."

We don't have to be a crumb in a crumbling world. We have too much going for us. The fact is, God is in control of the confusion. His wise providence and His gracious mercy are only a prayer away.

What's more, we have God's promises right at hand. Look for the good news in God's Word. Search for the eternal wisdom in the face of earthly adversity. Take a great big drink from the water that never runs dry, even when we are walking through the desert. The news is mostly good. God has promised to equip you for the journey up your mountain. And He'll not only equip you, He'll go with you.

You *can* survive!

God Created the World in Six Days and Did Not Once Ask My Advice!

(Letting God Take Control of the Situation)

Perhaps you've heard the story about the pastor who went to his church office on Monday morning and discovered a dead mule in the churchyard. After much thought, he decided to call the local sheriff. Since there did not appear to be any foul play, the sheriff recommended that the pastor call the local health authorities.

The health director indicated that there was no immediate health threat and told him to call the sanitation department. The sanitation director told him that he could not pick up the mule without authorization from the mayor.

Unfortunately, the pastor knew the mayor and was not excited about calling him. The mayor had a bad temper and was known to be difficult to deal with.

Finally, the pastor mustered the courage to call the mayor. The mayor immediately began to rant and rave and finally said, "Why did you call me anyway? Isn't it your job to bury the dead?"

The pastor, collecting his thoughts, paused for a brief prayer and asked the Lord to direct his response. He then said, "Mayor, it is my job to bury the dead, but I always like to notify the next of kin first!"[5]

Our world is so full of red tape and rules. (It seems to me, some folks just like to be in charge.) We've all met people who act like vice-chairmen of Heaven's board of directors. They're usually the ones with answers to questions that haven't even been asked. When they toot their own horns, they do it through a hundred-watt sound system.

Control freaks—they get up during the night for fear that the Lord might fall asleep and not leave anyone in charge. Others simply want to take control of every situation according to their particular (and, of course, correct) ideas about things. My wife, Linda, and I encountered just such a person in Nashville, Tennessee.

Several years ago, while living in Nashville, we decided to take a tour of the city. The bus driver carefully noted the various Civil War battle sites of Nashville. He said, "Look out the right side of the bus. It was on that spot that a small group of Confederate soldiers held off a whole Yankee brigade." Driving on a few blocks, he said, "It was at this exact location a fifteen-year-old Confederate boy whipped a whole Yankee platoon by himself!"

As the bus driver continued to wax eloquent, a man from New York City asked, "What about the Yankees? Didn't they win anything at the battle of Nashville?"

The bus driver responded, "Not as long as I'm giving this tour!"

"I'M IN CHARGE HERE, I THINK."

Following the assassination attempt on President Reagan, esteemed military General and Chief of Staff Alexander Haig

52

addressed the nation. He tried to reassure the country in the wake of the unsettling events by telling us that everything was under control, that he was in charge. You may remember the sudden firestorm that resulted in what seemed to be a breach in the presidential chain of command. It didn't take very long for General Haig to realize that he wasn't exactly the commander-in-chief! He had more *scrambled eggs* on his face than he did on his general's cap.

When the buzzards start circlin' overhead, one of the first tendencies is to try to take charge of the situation.

Job tried it. This Old Testament character was president and CEO of CALAMITY, INC. The Bible says Satan asked for, and was granted, permission to try a faithful servant of the Lord named Job. The trials were almost beyond comprehension. His children perished when their house fell on them. His livestock and servants were destroyed by fire. And finally, he was stricken with painful boils. But he remained steadfast in his faith—for a while. *"In all this, Job did not sin in what he said"* (Job 2:10).

Soon, a committee of "friends" came to visit. They had all the joviality of a squad of cheerleaders at an embalming school! And after a moment of silence (that lasted seven days), they began to dialogue with Job over his circumstances. "It's because of your sin," Job's bad-mouthing buddies insisted.

"Not so," Job retorted. And the war of words raged on.

Realizing he had completely lost control of his world, Job's bitterness began to surface. He said, *"I cry out to you, O God, but you do not answer; I stand up, but you merely look at me"* (Job 30:20). In one sentence, Job pronounced sentence on the Almighty: "You aren't listening, and even if You are, You sure aren't doing much about it!"

Good place for Job to step in and take control, right? Wrong!

The answer echoed from Heaven. *"Where were you when I laid the earth's foundation? Tell me, if you understand. Who marked off its dimensions?"* (Job 38:4-5). God reminds Job that from the beginning He had the world and everything in it under perfect control. Nothing here was happening by accident. Job couldn't measure the dimensions of this problem any more than he could measure the planet with a yardstick. But God had measured it. His grace was deep and wide enough to keep Job safe in this calamity.

> *If all difficulties were known at the outset of a long journey, most of us would never start out at all.*
> —*Dan Rather*

"GIVE ME THAT REMOTE!"

Some of earth's greatest struggles don't take place on the battlefield or in the corporate boardroom. They take place in the family room with strife over the remote control. If someone doesn't like one of the 225 available satellite channels, the war is on! It's a battle of the wills, usually won by the person who has had the satellite dish installed (or the one who makes the monthly cable television payments).

Oh, the power of channel surfing! With a click of a finger, a sad movie with a million-dollar budget can be replaced with a low-budget, senseless comedy. Job needed a remote to cope with his situation, which wasn't exactly a Disney World experience. As Job struggled with the questions of his heart, he longed to change the channel. In fact, he probably wanted to hit the rewind button and bring back his former life.

When Job began to question God, his tongue was in high gear—but his brain was still on a slow charge! *"Then the LORD answered Job out of the storm. He said: 'Who is this that darkens my counsel with words without knowledge?'"* (Job 38:1-3). Toler Translation: "You've done it again, Job. You've assumed that I have relinquished control of this situation!" Job didn't have a clue as to who was holding the remote.

Before we go finger-pointing, let's remember the times we've grabbed the remote and tried to wrest control of a crisis from the hands of the Creator. Why did we do that? There are several reasons:

PRIDE

Sometimes we actually think we can do a better job than God. That's built into us at the factory, like an automatic transmission. It was pride that caused the devil to stand against the throne of Heaven. He actually thought he could do a better job of running the universe. The deceit of sin is that it makes us believe we don't need heavenly help. Instead of saying, "In God We Trust," we end up saying, "In Ourselves We Trust."

My lifelong friend David Vaughn once gave this sterling reminder to me:

Never Trust a Dentist That . . .

Wears dentures.

Has hairy knuckles.

*Has a drill driven by a system of pulleys
connected to three mice on a treadmill.*

Sends you a Christmas card and then bills you for it.

Chews tobacco and spits it in the sink.

Uses the suction hose to empty your pockets.

We are required to put our trust in other people, like medical professionals, and we often do so readily. Yet when a crisis comes, we rarely put our trust in the most qualified "Professional," our sovereign God. Instead, we tend to reach out to human institutions or human technologies. In the process, we thwart His efforts to help us to mature and grow.

"You are the master of your own fate," the enemy of our soul speaks. But this enemy doesn't hold the remote.

DISCOURAGEMENT

There are times when daily living is like wearing a cement overcoat. It just gets heavier as the day wears on. Job felt that way after a while. Other great biblical characters struggled with discouragement. For example, the psalmist David, composer of hundreds of songs, forgot the melody at times. He wrote, *"Why are you downcast, O my soul? Why so disturbed within me? Put your hope in God, for I will yet praise him, my Savior and my God. My soul is downcast within me; therefore I will remember you from the land of the Jordan"* (Psalm 42:5-6). He seems to bounce back and forth from the major to the minor key—just like the lady in this story:

Dr. Lee Noel, consultant in education with the University of Pennsylvania, tells of a lecture series he gave in New York, where he had spoken several times before. He first spoke there in 1982, and then ten years later his schedule had him back in that same area, speaking on a similar theme—excellence in education.

After one of the sessions, a lady approached him and did what you hope no person ever does to you. She wanted to know if he remembered her name. It had been ten years since he had met her. He'd had more than three hundred other speaking engagements since then, and now, some two million faces later, one lady was asking if he remembered her name!

He said, "As I looked at her, a little light went on in my mind, and to my own astonishment, her name popped right to the top of my mind."

"Yes, I do, I do remember your name," he said. "Your name is Eva Chastain." For a second she looked shocked. Then she said, "Well, yes, it *was* Eva Chastain. But I've gotten married since you saw me."

"Oh, I'm so happy," he followed. "Marriage is such a nice thing."

She jumped back in, "It's not that nice. My husband died."

57

"Oh, I'm so sorry," Dr. Noel said.

"Well, it's not that bad," she interrupted. "He left me a large insurance policy."

"Oh, that's good."

"No, it's not that good," she replied. "I built a house, and the house burned."

"Oh, I'm so sorry."

"Well, you don't have to feel sorry," she came back. "I had it insured for more than it was worth, and I built it back better than ever."

Dr. Noel said that every comment he made trying to "stay on the same page" with her, she flipped the page and kept him out of sequence for the entire conversation. Whatever he praised, she condemned, and whatever he felt sorry for, she figured up a way to make it wonderful. Up and down, back and forth. "By the end of that conversation," Dr. Noel said, "I was hoping I didn't have to talk with that lady again for at least ten more years."

He added, "Maybe by that time I will have forgotten her name for good!"[6]

Never go to a doctor whose office plants have died.
—Erma Bombeck

FEAR

We have so many phobias in our society that we sometimes feel like an outcast if we're not afraid of something. Fear is a powerful force. It can cause us to react in strange ways when we face buzzard-circling events.

The Sunday supplement magazine, *USA Weekend,* ran a cover story in its August 22-24, 1997, issue, titled "Fear: What Americans Are Afraid of Today." In a scientific poll, the magazine uncovered the things Americans fear most:

- 54% are "afraid" or "very afraid" of being in a car crash.
- 53% are "afraid" or "very afraid" of having cancer.
- 50% are "afraid" or "very afraid" of inadequate Social Security.
- 49% are "afraid" or "very afraid" of not having enough money for retirement.
- 36% are "afraid" or "very afraid" of food poisoning from meat.
- 35% are "afraid" or "very afraid" of getting Alzheimer's.
- 34% are "afraid" or "very afraid" of pesticides on food.
- 33% are "afraid" or "very afraid" of being a victim of individual violence.
- 32% are "afraid" or "very afraid" of being unable to pay current debts.
- 30% are "afraid" or "very afraid" of exposure to foreign viruses.
- 28% are "afraid" or "very afraid" of getting AIDS.
- 25% are "afraid" or "very afraid" of natural disasters.[7]

Dr. Paul Tournier observes that, "Fear creates what it fears. Fear of war impels a country to take the very measures which unleash war. The fear of losing the love of a loved one provokes us to just that lack of frankness which undermines love. The skier falls as soon as he begins to be afraid of falling. Fear of failing in an examination takes away the candidate's presence of mind and makes success more difficult."[8]

UNBELIEF

There are times when we try to take control of a crisis simply because we don't believe that God *can* take care of it. Jesus couldn't work miracles in His own hometown because of a prevailing unbelief. *"He did not do many miracles there because of their lack of faith"* (Matthew 13:58). The buzzards start circlin', and we grab for the promises of God's Word. But we hold them like a cheap cup of coffee from one of those rest-area machines—cautiously, with a fear of getting burned.

We've sung "Jesus loves me! This I know" from our earliest Sunday School days, but now we're not sure if He even likes us! We've prayed "God is great and God is good" over everything from baby food jars and PBJ sandwiches to petite sirloins, but when the buzzards are flying in formation over the wrecks of our life, we sometimes question His greatness and goodness. Unbelief causes us to grab for the remote.

REBELLION

Sometimes we try to take control just to prove a point. Isaiah the prophet says: *"All of us have become like one who is unclean, and all our righteous acts are like filthy rags; we all*

shrivel up like a leaf, and like the wind our sins sweep us away" (Isaiah 64:6).

Sometimes we abandon the good for the sake of a good gripe! Sometimes we just get into a sanctified snit. "This is no way to treat me! I'm a charter member of the First Church of the Dearly Departed!" We don't recognize that we are sinful and in need of God's grace. Because of our hardened hearts, we don't feel the tender touch of the Master in times of crisis.

God can't do anything for us when the bad times roll over us unless we let Him. He won't force His grace upon us. We have to be willing to hand Him the remote.

THE GREYHOUND PRINCIPLE

Greyhound buses have traversed the high roads and side roads of our land for decades. One of their classic commercials made an interesting plea: Relax, and leave the driving to us! It works—I've tried it.

I've climbed the steps of those Flexible or GM coaches, sat down in an overstuffed chair (and sometimes next to an overstuffed fellow passenger), closed my eyes to the concerns outside those big windows, and let the driver take me to my destination.

What if I had insisted on sitting next to the driver on his seat? Back then, I would have gotten a stern lecture. Today, I'd probably get jail time. No, I didn't buy my ticket to do the driving; I bought it to do the riding. The driver was certified. He was familiar with the route. The vehicle had been checked out. I was just along for the ride.

It may be that more people "fly the friendly skies" than ride the bumpy roads these days, but the principle is the same. If we're going to get to where we want to go, we're going to have to trust a professional. It's the Greyhound principle: Relax, and let the Lord take control and do the driving.

GIVE HIM THE DETAILS.

Jeanne Griffin, a member of my church, recently told me the story of a young woman, Brenda, who was invited to go rock climbing. Although she was scared to death, she went with her group to ascend a tremendous granite cliff. She put on the gear, took hold of the rope, and started up the face of the cliff.

After a while, she maneuvered to a ledge where she could take a breather. But as she was hanging there, the safety rope suddenly snapped against Brenda's eye, knocking out her contact lens. Standing precariously on the ledge, hundreds of feet above the ground, she began to look frantically for the lost lens. Hoping it had landed near her feet, she stooped down to search, patting the surface. It wasn't there. On that frail ledge between the summit and the ground, her sight now blurry, she grew more agitated and fearful. In desperation, she began to pray, asking the Lord to help her find the lens.

After reaching the summit, the group descended the mountain using a walking trail instead of rappelling down the

Top Ten Airline Announcements

10. Thank you for flying Delta Business Express. We hope you enjoyed giving us the business as much as we enjoyed taking you for a ride!

9. Your seat cushion can be used for flotation. In the event of an emergency water landing, please take the cushion—compliments of Reno Air.

8. Please use caution when opening the overhead bin. After a horrible landing like this, you can be certain your luggage has shifted.

7. As you exit, please remember—there may be fifty ways to leave your lover, but there are only four ways out of this airplane!

6. After a high-speed landing in Phoenix, "Whoa, big fella. Whoa!"

5. Welcome aboard Southwest Airlines. In the event of a sudden loss of cabin pressure, oxygen masks will descend from the ceiling. Stop screaming, and place it over your face.

4. Thanks for choosing TWA. We ask you to please remain seated as Captain Kangaroo bounces us to the terminal.

3. This is a nonsmoking flight. If you must smoke, please step out on the wing and watch our in-flight movie, *Gone with the Wind.*

2. Thank you for flying the friendly skies of United. Last one off the plane cleans it!

1. At American Airlines, we are pleased to have some of the best flight attendants in the industry. Unfortunately, none are on this flight.

same cliff. Brenda and the rest of her group soon met a party of climbers who were just beginning their ascent up the same cliff. One of them shouted out, "Hey, you guys! Anybody lose a contact lens?"

Brenda rushed toward the climber, elated. "How did you find it?" she asked excitedly. The climber told of seeing a tiny ant moving slowly across the large stone where he was sitting. As he looked closer, he noticed that the ant was carrying something. You guessed it—a contact lens!

You don't have to carry "this thing." If God can recruit an ant to carry a contact lens, He can take care of the details in your life.

CHANGE YOUR VIEWPOINT.

There's more than one way to look at a situation—even a buzzard-circlin' situation. Three people were visiting the Grand Canyon—a painter, a pastor, and a cowpoke. Looking over the massive canyon, each one verbalized his observation:

"Incredible!" the painter said. "I'd love to paint a picture of this!" The preacher waved his arms and cried, "Glory! Look what God has done!"

The cowboy exclaimed, "I'd sure hate to lose a cow down there!"

What do you see when you look at your situation? An illustration of God's handiwork, or just someplace to lose a cow?

Someone sent me a story that drove this point home.

The carpenter I hired to help me restore an old farm-house had just finished a rough first day on the job. A flat tire made him lose an hour of work; his electric saw quit; and now his ancient pickup truck refused to start. While I drove him home, he sat in stony silence.

On arriving, he invited me in to meet his family. As we walked toward the front door, he paused briefly at a small tree, touching the tips of the branches with both hands. When opening the door, he underwent an amazing transformation. His tanned face was wreathed in smiles, and he hugged his two small children and gave his wife a kiss.

Afterward, he walked me to the car. We passed the tree, and my curiosity got the better of me. I asked him about what I had seen him do earlier.

"Oh, that's my trouble tree," he replied. "I know I can't help having troubles on the job, but one thing's for sure—troubles don't belong in the house with my wife and the children. So I just hang them up on the tree every night when I come home. Then in the morning, I pick them up again. Funny thing is," he smiled, "when I come out in the morning to pick them up, there ain't nearly as many as I remember hanging up the night before."

Some folks look at a tree and see an object that blocks the sunlight. They envision the leaves that will fall from it and clutter the ground beneath. They see the bark of the tree and think of its coldness and hardness.

65

Other folks look at a tree and see its beauty. Its winter death is a promise of spring. Its summer green foliage is a lovely prelude to autumn reds and gold. Some see a place where they can hang their troubles. The same tree—yet how it appears depends on how you look at it.

Paul said, *"Whatever is true, whatever is noble, whatever is right, whatever is pure, whatever is lovely, whatever is admirable—if anything is excellent or praiseworthy—think about such things"* (Philippians 4:8).

If you want your ship to come in, you must first build a dock!
—Mark Gilroy

Release your death grip. Jesus gave us a wonderful invitation: *"Come to me, all you who are weary and burdened, and I will give you rest. Take my yoke upon you and learn from me, for I am gentle and humble in heart, and you will find rest for your souls"* (Matthew 11:28-29). He invites us to trade the things that bind us for the things that free us.

A story is told about Toad and Frog (written by Arnold Lobel and adapted by yours truly):

One day, Toad baked some cookies. "These cookies smell very good," said Toad. He ate one. "They taste even better," he said. Then Toad ran to Frog's house. "Frog! Frog!" cried Toad, "Taste these cookies!"

Frog ate one of the cookies and said, "These are the best cookies I have ever eaten." Soon Frog and

Toad sat down together and started to eat the whole plate of cookies.

"You know, Toad," said Frog, with his mouth full of cookies, "I think we should stop eating. We will soon be sick."

"You're right!" said Toad. "Let's eat one last cookie, and then we'll stop." So Frog and Toad ate another cookie.

Looking at the cookies left on the plate, Toad said, "Frog, let's eat just one more, and then we'll stop!"

"Good idea!" Frog replied, reaching for another. "We need some self-control."

"What's that?" asked Toad.

Frog answered, "Self-control is trying hard not to do something that you really want to do."

"You mean like trying not to eat all these cookies?" asked Toad.

"Right," said Frog, putting the last two in the box. "There! Now we won't eat any more cookies."

"But we can always open the box," said Toad.

"That's true," said Frog. So he tied some string around the box. "There," he said. "Now we will not be able to eat any more."

"But we can always cut the string and open the box!" said Toad.

"That's also true," said Frog. So he got a ladder and put the box of remaining cookies up on a high shelf. "There," said Frog, "now we won't be able to eat any more."

Toad spoke up, "But we can climb the ladder, take the box down from the shelf, cut the string, and open the box."

Exasperated, Frog answered, "I guess you're right about that as well!"

So Frog climbed the ladder, took down the box from the shelf, cut the string, and opened the box. Then he took the lid off the box, carried it outside, and shouted, "Hey, birds! Here's some cookies!" Birds came from everywhere. They picked up the remaining cookies in their beaks and flew away.

"Now we don't have any more cookies," said Toad sadly. "Not even one."

"Yes," said Frog, "but we have lots and lots of willpower!"

"You can keep your willpower," said Toad. "I'm gonna go home and bake me some cookies!"[9]

That's a long road to a very important question: What are you holding in your hand that you need to feed to the birds?

LET CHRIST RULE OVER THE CRISIS.

The only way Job could get a sense of relief over the awful situations of his life was simply to surrender. Job 42:1-3 says, *"Then Job replied to the LORD: 'I know that you can do all things; no plan of yours can be thwarted. You asked, "Who is this that obscures my counsel without knowledge?" Surely I spoke of things I did not understand, things too wonderful for me to know.'"* Toler translation: "I surrender, Lord! I've had my tongue in *D* and my brain in *N*. Now I'm going to put both of them in *P*. I'm not moving until You tell me to!"

We'll never be able to surrender control of those buzzard-circlin' situations until we have a coronation ceremony—until we decide to let the Lord Jesus Christ rule over the kingdom of our calamities. Like the old hymn, we'll declare, "King of my life, I crown Thee now; Thine shall the glory be."[10] The apostle Paul knew that kind of surrender. He said, *"I have been crucified with Christ and I no longer live, but Christ lives in me. The life I live in the body, I live by faith in the Son of God"* (Galatians 2:20).

SHALL I TRUST GOD TO HANDLE THIS SITUATION
(OR SHALL I TRUST MYSELF)?

Some things are as plain as a pout on a pit bull. We don't have the inner resources to walk past a wall with a "WET PAINT" sign on it without sneaking a touch. How can we ever stay calm amidst a calamity in our own strength? The good news is, we don't have to. Job finally got it! He couldn't form the foundations of the world; he couldn't measure the planets; and he couldn't quiet that bunch of amateur counselors.

All he could do was lay himself down on the green grass of God's wonderful wisdom and rest. God's Word reminds us, *"Do not forget my teaching, but keep my commands in your heart, for they will prolong your life many years and bring you prosperity. Let love and faithfulness never leave you; bind them around your neck, write them on the tablet of your heart. Then you will win favor and a good name in the sight of God and man. Trust in the LORD with all your heart and lean not on your own understanding"* (Proverbs 3:1-5). We must accept the future by faith, one day at a time.

My old friend Chuck Crow tells the story of the little boy who went to his dad's room one night. The boy's mother was away, and he was scared to sleep by himself; so his dad invited him to crawl in bed with him. After the lights had been out for a while and they were lying there in the dark, the little boy said, "Daddy, is your face looking this way?"

"Yes, son, I'm facing your direction."

"Good, Daddy," he said. "Just stay that way 'til I go to sleep."

You can face your midnight hours. You can face your fears. The buzzards may be circlin', but the God of the universe is looking in your direction.

Trust involves letting go and knowing God will catch you.
—*James Dobson*

PSALM 8

> *O LORD, our Lord, how majestic is your name in all the earth! You have set your glory above the heavens. From the lips of children and infants you have ordained praise because of your enemies, to silence the foe and the avenger. When I consider your heavens, the*

work of your fingers, the moon and the stars, which you have set in place, what is man that you are mindful of him, the son of man that you care for him? You made him a little lower than the heavenly beings and crowned him with glory and honor. You made him ruler over the works of your hands; you put everything under his feet: all flocks and herds, and the beasts of the field, the birds of the air, and the fish of the sea, all that swim the paths of the seas. O LORD, our Lord, how majestic is your name in all the earth!

Hold the Phone! Can't We Talk about This First, Lord?

(God Uses Testing Times as Building Times)

One of my favorite television shows as a teen was *The Fugitive*. Perhaps it was my awareness of the relationship between the Sam Sheppard story and the television program that captivated my attention. Like most fans of the program, I was thrilled when they released the movie about the elusive fugitive. While watching the movie, I couldn't help but think about another famous "fugitive"—Moses.

Moses was an Israelite who was adopted and raised with all the wealth and privilege of the Egyptian pharaoh's house. Pharaoh, seeing that the Israelites were multiplying in number and strength, set slave masters over them and assigned them to hard labor. One day, when Moses was a grown man, he came upon a fellow Israelite who was being beaten by an Egyptian. Moses was angry and, in defense of the Israelite, struck and killed the soldier. Pharaoh was furious and wanted to kill Moses. So Moses, true to fugitive form, took off. He went to live in Midian, met and married the daughter of a religious leader (a preacher's kid), and settled for a life of sheepherding.

One day, an angel of the Lord appeared to him disguised as a bush—a burning bush at that! When he saw that the bush was on fire but didn't burn up, he uttered one of the great "Duh!" statements in history: *"I will go over and see this strange sight"* (Exodus 3:3). Actually, the Lord was using the bush as a multimedia presentation. The awesome sight was soon replaced with an awesome sound. The Lord called to Moses out of the burning bush:

> *"I am the God of your father, the God of Abraham, the God of Isaac and the God of Jacob." At this, Moses hid his face, because he was afraid to look at God.*
>
> *The LORD said, "I have indeed seen the misery of my people in Egypt. I have heard them crying out because of their slave drivers, and I am concerned about their suffering. So I have come down to rescue them from the hand of the Egyptians and to bring them up out of that land into a good and spacious land, a land flowing with milk and honey. . . . The cry of the Israelites has reached me, and I have seen the way the Egyptians are oppressing them. So now, go. I am sending you to Pharaoh to bring my people the Israelites out of Egypt."*

Exodus 3:6-10

Did you notice that? God said, "I have seen the way the Egyptians are oppressing them." God has an eye on the events of our lives. He not only saw His people's problems, but He was going to do something about them.

The faithful fugitive got the message: God wants me to quit tending *sheep* and start tending *people*—multiplied thousands of them. As nervous as a cockroach at a bug-exterminator convention, Moses replied, *"Who am I, that I should go to Pharaoh and bring the Israelites out of Egypt?"* (Exodus 3:11). In other words, "Hold the phone! Can't we talk about this first, Lord?"

76

God reassured him, *"I will be with you"* (Exodus 3:12). That was good enough for Moses (and it ought to be good enough for us). The next pages of biblical history are filled with the awesome tests and triumphs of this great leader. He endured, leading the Israelites out of Egypt on a wilderness journey toward the Promised Land. The tests far outnumbered the triumphs. He suffered through more complaints than compliments, more disheartening than delight, and more rebellion than recognition. But he kept going with more determination than that pink bunny in the battery commercials.

You'll also remember that the Promised Land journey was filled with some colossal calamities. Walking with God has never exempted His people from a trial or two. In 1837, one well-known college refused entrance to young ladies who couldn't "kindle a fire, wash potatoes, and repeat the multiplication table and at least two-thirds of the shorter catechism." The multiplication table and the catechism requirements alone would eliminate many of this year's freshman class! But when you add the next requirement, it puts all of us in a pickle: "Every member of the school shall walk a mile a day unless a fresher, earthquake, or some other calamity prevents."[11]

Like the times when we're trying to get in a morning walk and that neighbor's Doberman gets loose, calamities put a stumble in our step. In fact, calamity is as common as a cold—and just as much of a nuisance.

How we *face* calamity is where it gets interesting. Have you ever gone through a trying time and wondered, *What in the world did the Lord have in mind when He allowed this?* The Bible gives us a definitive answer: He has nothing but our good in mind. *"Consider it pure joy, my brothers, whenever you face trials of many kinds, because you know that the testing of your faith develops perseverance. Perseverance must finish its work so that you may be mature and complete, not lacking any-thing"* (James 1:2-4).

God allows the buzzard-circlin' times in our lives to develop us, not to destroy us. Isaiah the prophet explained that God uses unusual means, means beyond our comprehension, to bring about His loving purposes. God says in Isaiah 55:8-9, *"'My thoughts are not your thoughts, neither are your ways my ways,' declares the LORD. 'As the heavens are higher than the earth, so are my ways higher than your ways and my thoughts than your thoughts.'"*

MONDAY MOURNING

Often, Monday is the first day of the w-e-a-k! We survived the Friday drive time. We squeaked by the Saturday "circus." We made our devotional dent in the Lord's house on Sunday. But *"Heeeere's* Monday!" Back to the realities of life. The pace increases while our strength decreases. Back to the office grind. Back to the relationship wars. Back to the insecurities and uncertainties of the nine-to-fives and the Monday-through-Fridays of our lives.

Monday is a not-so-gentle reminder of what life is really all about. Adam's disobedience sealed it. God pronounced the sentence for Adam's sinfulness: *"By the sweat of your brow you will eat your food until you return to the ground, since from it*

you were taken; for dust you are and to dust you will return"
(Genesis 3:19).

Adam and Eve abandoned the Garden of Eden for a spiritual desert, and they dragged us along like a cat being trained to walk on a leash. We got the short end of the inheritance.

Pain.

Tears.

Sorrow.

Loss.

Heartbreak.

Trials invaded humanity like a sudden summer storm, but God loved us too much to leave us out in the rain. He made a provision: He would use many of these trials to toughen us.

> *God is a humorist. If you have any doubts about it,*
> *look in the mirror.*
> —*Ken Olson*

1. Trials propel us.

Many pastors' trials come not on Monday, but on Sunday. One pastor had been agonizing over how he was going to ask the congregation to come up with more money than they were expecting to give for repairs to the church building. He was consumed by the situation. Upon his arrival at church on Sunday morning, he was irritated to experience yet one more difficulty. The regular organist was sick, and a substitute had been brought in at the last minute. The substitute organist (who played the organ at the minor-league baseball park) asked what he should play for the worship service.

"Here's a copy of the service," responded the pastor. "But you'll have to think of something to play after I make the announcement about church finances."

At the appropriate time in the service, the pastor paused and said, "Brothers and sisters, we are in great difficulty. The roof repairs cost twice as much as we expected, and we need $4,000 more. I want everyone who will pledge at least $100 to please stand up."

Being a quick thinker, the substitute organist played "The Star-Spangled Banner." Everyone stood! Only in the realm of grace could an annoying situation turn into a great blessing! (That's how the substitute organist became the regular church organist.)

John Claypool reminds us of God's transforming power in a geography lesson about the Dead Sea in Israel. He says, "The Dead Sea is appropriately named. Nothing grows or lives in it. The consistency of the water is like none other in the world. Its only outlet is evaporation, so heavily concentrated compounds remain after the water is lifted to the sky. The potential of such a lake seems limited. To the contrary, engineers estimate that if the potash around the Dead Sea could be mixed and distributed, there would be enough fertilizer created to supply the whole surface of the earth for at least five years. Some people or situations feel like dead ends. Allow God to help you see the potential that your eyes may be missing."[12]

There is potential in problems. If we let them, problems propel us forward. In times of crisis, we move closer to God.

We gain a clearer understanding of His promises. Moses did. Leading the children of Israel from the pursuing armies of Pharaoh, he arrived at the shore of the Red Sea. What happened next is a great lesson. Instead of taking the Israelites *around,* God took them *through.* Exodus 14:21-22: *"Moses stretched out his hand over the sea, and all that night the LORD drove the sea back with a strong east wind and turned it into dry land. The waters were divided, and the Israelites went through the sea on dry ground, with a wall of water on their right and on their left."* As the Israelites continued to move toward God, they continued to experience miracles.

2. Trials perfect us.

The psalmist David learned about the no-pain, no-gain principle in his own crisis. He says, *"It was good for me to be afflicted so that I might learn your decrees. The law from your mouth is more precious to me than thousands of pieces of silver and gold"* (Psalm 119:71-72). His trials drove him to God's Word, where he found comfort and wisdom—where he caught a glimpse of those things that needed to be surrendered to the sovereign God.

Trials are the classrooms where the lessons of faith are best taught on the blackboard of God's Word. Case in point: Exodus 14:31. It says, *"When the Israelites saw the great power the LORD displayed against the Egyptians, the people feared the LORD and put their trust in him and in Moses his servant."*

3. Trials empower us.

The New Testament apostle Paul made an interesting observation. He said, *"We also rejoice in our sufferings, because we know that suffering produces perseverance; perseverance, character; and character, hope"* (Romans 5:3-4). This spiritual principle can be seen in the physical realm as well. Many in our society work out, including weight lifting as part of their regimens. What we want from our efforts are results—better, healthier, more muscular bodies. Yet we don't get those results by watching an early morning television exercise program while holding a jelly doughnut in one hand and the remote in the other. Without the pumping of iron, there is no protruding of muscles. And spiritually mature muscles come from "exercising" through trials and tribulations. The Israelites were toughened by their trek through the wilderness. Moses knew it was going to be a tough trip, but he also knew that it would toughen the troops.

We often argue with God about our adversities, saying, "Can't we talk about this first, Lord?" But those buzzard-circlin' events are the very things that build us—that make us stronger.

Greatness is not determined by what it takes to get a man going—greatness is determined by what it takes to stop a man.
—*Anonymous*

"'TIS SO SWEET TO TRUST IN JESUS."

The nineteenth-century hymn writer Lousia M.R. Stead put music to the message of what it's like to trust God in the midst of our trials:

'Tis so sweet to trust in Jesus, just to take Him at His Word;

Just to rest upon His promise; just to know, "Thus saith the Lord."

Jesus, Jesus, how I trust Him! How I've proved Him o'er and o'er!

Jesus, Jesus, precious Jesus! O for grace to trust Him more!

If it weren't for the rigors of life, we never would understand the wonders of a relationship with God. Trials build trust. Moses led the congregation in singing a praise chorus after the Red Sea incident:

Then Moses and the Israelites sang this song to the LORD:

"I will sing to the LORD,
for he is highly exalted.

The horse and its rider
he has hurled into the sea.

The LORD is my strength and my song;
he has become my salvation.

He is my God, and I will praise him,
my father's God, and I will exalt him."

Exodus 15:1-2

They didn't need to project those words on the side of a mountain with a Power Point slide presentation. They knew them because they had experienced them.

God can be trusted in times of temptation. Moses later wrote about that when the Israelites were settling in: *"The eternal God is your refuge, and underneath are the everlasting*

arms. He will drive out your enemy before you, saying, 'Destroy him!'" (Deuteronomy 33:27).

The word "refuge" is better rendered as "dwelling place." The children of Israel needed to be reminded that even though they were homeless and their national future was uncertain, they were in the presence and security of the eternal God. Ultimately, this is the only thing that matters. Outside His refuge, the world is an empty, lonely place.

I'LL TRADE YOU.

I remember my "trading days." As a child, I would give up a treasured baseball card, for example, in exchange for an even greater treasure—marbles. It wasn't exactly Wall Street, but some of those trades turned out to be pretty good investments. Trusting God in times of crisis is a good investment of our spiritual energies. When we trade with Him, we always get the better end of the deal.

> *Be still, and know that I am God; I will be exalted among the nations, I will be exalted in the earth.*

> Psalm 46:10

WHEN WE PUT OUR TRUST IN GOD,
HE GIVES US HIS PRESENCE IN PLACE OF EMPTINESS.

Moses cried out to God after the tempest that surrounded the giving of the Ten Commandments. "Hold the phone! I thought we had an agreement!" Later, Moses reaffirmed His trust in the Lord, and the Lord calmed his spirit with a promise. *"My Presence will go with you, and I will give you rest"* (Exodus 33:14).

Carl Jung, Swiss psychiatrist and founder of the school of analytical psychology, stated that "the central neurosis of our time is the sense of emptiness." This is why men and women seek to satisfy themselves with drugs, alcohol, work, pleasure seeking, and things of that nature. The true refuge of peace and rest is God!

WHEN WE PUT OUR TRUST IN GOD,
HE GIVES US HIS SECURITY IN PLACE OF UNREST.

Moses, alone on that mountain, would have been totally insecure—a frightened man—but God had been with him every step, even to the hour of death. The Bible says, *"The LORD gives strength to his people; the LORD blesses his people with peace"* (Psalm 29:11). Moses found that to be true, as has everyone who has put a shaking hand in the hand of the Heavenly Father. It's a rest that the world cannot understand. Jesus promised us a permanent peace in an unsteady world: *"Peace I leave with you; my peace I give you. I do not give to you as the world gives. Do not let your hearts be troubled and do not be afraid"* (John 14:27).

WHEN WE PUT OUR TRUST IN GOD,
HE GIVES US HIS ANSWERS IN HIS TIME.

From the very beginning, Moses had some gigantic questions about his assignment to be the leader of Israel. As a contestant on the television game show, *Jeopardy,* Moses might have said, "I'll take 'Questions I'd Like to Ask God' for five hundred dollars, Alex." Moses pled with God, saying, *"What if they do not believe me or listen to me and say, 'The LORD did not appear to you'?"* (Exodus 4:1). The Lord replied with a question in Exodus 4:2-5, saying:

> *"What is that in your hand?"*
>
> *"A staff," he replied.*
>
> *The LORD said, "Throw it on the ground."*
>
> *Moses threw it on the ground and it became a snake, and he ran from it. Then the LORD said to him, "Reach out your hand and take it by the tail." So Moses reached out and took hold of the snake and it turned back into a staff in his hand. "This," said the LORD, "is so that they may believe that the LORD, the God of their fathers—the God of Abraham, the God of Isaac and the God of Jacob—has appeared to you."*

God didn't put the whole puzzle together. He just handed Moses enough pieces to meet the demands of the day. Learning to accept God's answers, in God's time and in God's way, is a vital part of the building process.

WHEN WE PUT OUR TRUST IN GOD,
HE GIVES US PROMISE IN THE MIDST OF OUR PREDICAMENTS.

Another part of the building process is faith. God's final answers are beyond time. He didn't say we wouldn't have problems here on earth. But He did say that one day we would be through with problems.

And our faith in that promise keeps us going. Jesus said, *"Do not let your hearts be troubled. Trust in God; trust also in me. In my Father's house are many rooms; if it were not so, I would have told you. I am going there to prepare a place for you. And if I go and prepare a place for you, I will come back and take you to be with me that you also may be where I am"* (John 14:1-3).

There are many "rooms" in the Father's house. And they will all feel like home. Here, we set up tents in a land of trouble. These days are about as stable as a two-hundred-dollar Christmas tree on a twenty-cent tree stand. Isn't it amazing how much of our holiday is spent adjusting that tree! One somersault by one grandchild can cause one fine mess. Like those Christmas tree adjustments, we may spend our days trying to keep things in balance.

But God has the balancing act well under control. He may even use momentary imbalances to build us up. After spending some dangerous moments in an intensive care unit, Kenneth Rogers, a leader in my church, told me with tears in his eyes, "Pastor, I thought it was the end for me, but when it looks like you're finished, God is just beginning!"

You may trust the Lord too little,
but you can never trust Him too much.
—Anonymous

DO YOU PROVIDE BENEFITS?

One of the first questions a job applicant usually asks concerns company benefits. What a company offers in its benefits package has a great bearing on our level of interest in a position and the level of security within the job. Better benefits often mean a better company that is willing to look out for its own.

God's benefits are proactive and far outweigh any others. For example, as someone has said, "The retirement plan is out of this world!" But the greatest benefit is God's personal involvement with His people. It's as if the wisdom, wealth, and power of the CEO of a Fortune 500 company are written in as a benefit to one of his or her employees! Just imagine it. The first-year mail clerk has the same rights and privileges as the head of the company. That may not catch on at Microsoft, but it's a done deal for the child of God!

Not long ago, Dr. Bill Bright, founder of Campus Crusade for Christ, sent me a copy of the manuscript for his new book, *Discovering God.* In his humble manner, Dr. Bright asked me to write an endorsement for the book. That may have been the easiest thing I've ever done! After reading it, I immediately recorded the following statements about God, taken from Dr. Bright's book, in my daily study Bible. Each day I read the following trust-building statements about God:

1. Because God is a personal Spirit . . . I will seek intimate fellowship with Him.

2. Because God is all-powerful . . . He can help me with anything.

3. Because God is ever-present . . . He is always with me.

4. Because God knows everything . . . I will go to Him with all of my questions and concerns.

5. Because God is sovereign . . . I will joyfully submit to His will.

6. Because God is holy . . . I will devote myself to Him in purity, worship, and service.

7. Because God is absolute truth . . . I will believe what He says and live accordingly.

8. Because God is righteous . . . I will live by His standards.

9. Because God is just . . . He will always treat me fairly.

10. Because God is love . . . He is unconditionally committed to my well-being.

11. Because God is merciful . . . He forgives me of my sins when I sincerely confess them.

12. Because God is faithful . . . I will trust Him to always keep His promises.

13. Because God never changes . . . my future is secure and eternal.[13]

In a *Moody Monthly* magazine article, Bonnie Perry wrote about the tragedy one family faced when the husband became addicted to the Internet. As his involvement with the Web widened, his interest in his family narrowed. Soon the family unit dissolved. Perry said, "Sometimes our dreams don't die in a moment, they dissipate slowly—like a glittering fireworks display that lingers before it succumbs to the darkness."[14]

Tragedies may not come as slowly. A tragedy may come like a tornado to a sleeping town. Suddenly, everything is different. But whether they are sudden or gradual, the buzzard-circlin' times of our lives can build us up rather than tear us apart—if we let God use them for our benefit and for His glory.

Leaning on the Everlasting Arms

What a fellowship, what a joy divine,
Leaning on the everlasting arms!
What a blessedness, what a peace is mine,
Leaning on the everlasting arms!

What have I to dread, what have I to fear,
Leaning on the everlasting arms?
I have blessed peace with my Lord so near,
Leaning on the everlasting arms.

Leaning, leaning,
Safe and secure from all alarms;
Leaning, leaning,
Leaning on the everlasting arms.

—Elisha A. Hoffman, 1839-1929

Chapter 5

When the Fountain of Youth Has Rusted

(Learning to Cope with Life's Challenges)

*Walk in all the way that the L*ORD *your God has commanded you, so that you may live and prosper and prolong your days in the land that you will possess.*

Deuteronomy 5:33

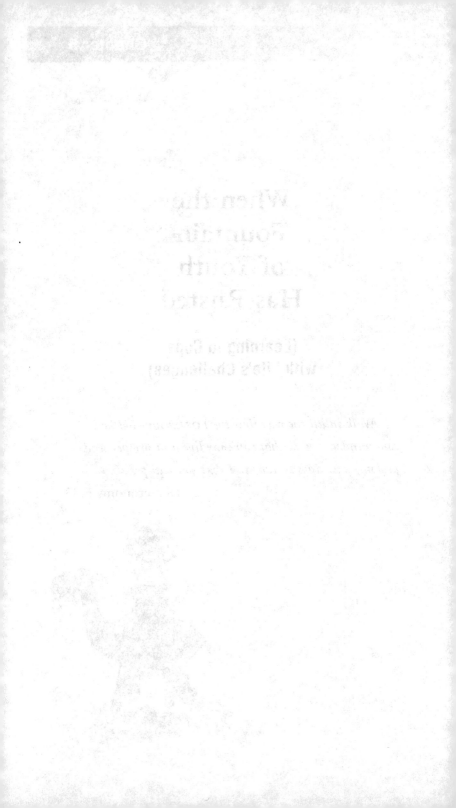

Buzzard-circlin' times aren't age specific. In life, there's no sign that says, "You must be this tall to go on this ride." We're all candidates for a calamity or two. Sometimes a little rust works its way into the fountain of youth.

So, it's not *whether* we face those turbulent times but rather *how* we face them that will make the difference in our lives.

A man went to the doctor after weeks of symptoms. The doctor examined him carefully, then called the patient's wife into his office.

"Your husband is suffering from a rare form of anemia. Without treatment, he'll be dead in a few weeks. The good news is, it can be treated with proper nutrition.

"You will need to get up early every morning and fix your husband a hot breakfast—pancakes, bacon and eggs, the works. He'll need a home-cooked lunch every day and then a seven-course dinner every evening.

"Also, his immune system is weak, so your home must be kept spotless. Do you want to break the news, or shall I?" asked the doctor.

"I will," the wife replied.

She walked into the exam room. The husband asked, "What did the doctor say?"

With a sob, she blurted out, "The doctor says you're gonna die!"[15]

If anyone should have been counted out, it should have been the New Testament apostle Paul. This renowned Bible character, raised in privilege and educated in the finest Hebrew schools, became a raging activist who vowed to wipe Christianity from the face of the earth.

Instead, he met Christ.

On the road to another killing, imprisoning, or beating of Christians, Paul met Jesus. In an instant, he switched teams. He fell "victim" to the mercy and grace of a risen Savior. From then on, he marched arm in arm and heart to heart with the very people he once despised.

And the journey didn't get easier. Paul the *persecutor* soon became Paul the *persecuted*. The very faith he once hated soon became the focal point of his enemy's hatred. He was always about a "stone's throw" away from the trauma center!

I have worked much harder, been in prison more frequently, been flogged more severely, and been exposed to death again and again. Five times I received from the Jews the forty lashes minus one. Three times I was beaten with rods, once I was stoned, three times I was shipwrecked, I spent a night and a day in the open sea, I have been constantly on the move. I have been in danger from rivers, in danger from bandits, in danger from my own countrymen, in danger from Gentiles; in danger in the city, in danger in the country, in danger at sea; and in danger from false brothers. I have labored and toiled

and have often gone without sleep; I have known hunger
and thirst and have often gone without food; I have been
cold and naked.

2 Corinthians 11:23-27

Sound like someone we'd like to hang out with? Actually, we're closer to him than we might think. Many of those adversities have been ours—at least in part. Maybe we haven't done jail time, but we know what it is to be imprisoned by a physical or emotional infirmity. Maybe we haven't been ship-wrecked, but we know what it's like to be tossed around by the storms of life.

We've known dangers.

We've been beaten up verbally.

We've been the subjects of lies.

We've labored in vain.

We've gone without sleep.

We've felt the cold of loneliness.

We've felt the nakedness of vulnerability.

We are comrades with the fervent and persecuted Paul. And from this great apostle, we can learn how to cope with the very worst in the very best way.

WHEN I GROW UP, I WANT TO BE LIKE PAUL.

I have determined (it's recorded in my Palm Pilot), that someday I am going to grow up. Now, you can't prove that by my family and some of my friends—they think I've got a ways to go. But I have made up my mind that someday I will grow up! When I do, I want to be just like Paul.

Certainly, my life's goal is to be like the Christ whom Paul loved. But I also want to be like Paul who said, *"Follow my example, as I follow the example of Christ"* (1 Corinthians 11:1). Paul coped with difficult situations later in his life as much as he did in the beginning because his faith was anchored firmly in the power of a relationship with Christ. That's why I admire this apostle. It's the reason I've followed his example and, in the process, discovered his victory.

The apostle Paul is a poster child for victory over circumstances. But his positive attitude didn't come from the pages of an Anthony Robbins or Zig Ziglar best-seller. It came from his relationship with the Lord Jesus Christ. It came from a continuing realization of who he was, whose he was, and what was available to him for meeting the traumas of time.

JESUS IS THE ANSWER, BUT WHAT ARE THE QUESTIONS?

If you've read my book, *God's Never Failed Me, but He's Sure Scared Me to Death a Few Times,* you already know my life's journey has had a few speed bumps along the way. You'll also know that there are core values I have adopted—values that have sustained me during those calamitous days. They came from the godly teaching and example of my parents, from my Christian leaders, and from my Christian friends—people who have constantly directed me to the pages of the Bible. Wise King Solomon said, *"Remember your Creator in*

Top Ten Signs You're Growing More Mature

10. Your teeth spend the night in a jar.

9. You have an executive "lift" chair.

8. It takes you longer to go to sleep than it did to get tired.

7. You and the pharmacist are on a first-name basis.

6. It takes you twice as long to look half as nice.

5. The pressing question of your life is, "Where did I park the car?"

4. You get winded playing Bible Trivia.

3. You know all the answers, but nobody asks you the questions.

2. You walk with your head held high . . . to see through your bifocals.

1. Shuffleboard doesn't sound too bad.

the days of your youth, before the days of trouble come" (Ecclesiastes 12:1). I'm glad I got an early start!

Early on, I was taught that there are three major questions to be answered in life, questions that affected how I felt about myself and how I reacted to buzzard-circlin' times: First, "What shall I do with Christ?" Second, "Whom shall I marry?" And third, "What shall I do with my life?"

Derric Johnson, in *Lists, the Book,* said there are seven ages of man:

1. *At 20, he wants to wake up romantic.*

2. *At 30, he wants to wake up married.*

3. *At 40, he wants to wake up successful.*

4. *At 50, he wants to wake up rich.*

5. *At 60, he wants to wake up contented.*

6. *At 70, he wants to wake up healthy.*

7. *At 80, he wants to wake up!*[16]

On November 7, 2000, I woke up, and I suddenly realized that I had passed over into "age four." On that momentous day, I turned fifty years old. Coincidentally, it was Election Day. If I'd had my druthers, I wouldn't have voted for fifty. In fact, a few days later I felt like calling for a recount!

Now, I didn't wake up money-rich on my birthday, but I did reflect on the wealth of the last fifty years. I took some time to think about those three important questions I mentioned previously, and I realized that I wouldn't change any of my answers.

Remember: fifty isn't old if you're a tree!
—Anonymous

I also realized that coping with life's situations is as much about the spiritual and emotional as it is about the physical and financial. The same apostle wrote, *"Stand firm. Let nothing move you. Always give yourselves fully to the work of the Lord, because you know that your labor in the Lord is not in vain"* (1 Corinthians 15:58).

Now let's see how those three important questions affect how we cope with the buzzard- circlin' times.

1. "WHAT SHALL I DO WITH JESUS CHRIST?" (LEARNING TO COPE BEGINS WITH A GOOD ATTITUDE ABOUT OURSELVES.)

The primary issues of our lives are spiritual. If those issues are not settled, the traumas of time can very well send us over the edge. We were created to have fellowship with God. Being secure in that relationship, through faith in the Lord Jesus Christ, helps us through the rough times.

I have been able to get over some of the speed bumps in my life because, like Paul, I met Jesus. Every dimension of my life was forever changed the day He came into my life. My *past* was forgiven. My *present* was filled with purpose. And my *future* became a glorious hope that has not been hindered by the events of my life. Jesus said, *"Here I am! I stand at the door and knock. If anyone hears my voice and opens the door, I will come in"* (Revelation 3:20). The most important decision I ever made was to answer the door and invite Him in.

My relationship with Jesus Christ gave me an inner security, even when things around me were about as secure as a ceramic teapot on the bow of the Titanic. He gave me a good attitude about myself. Paul wrote, *"He redeemed us in order that the blessing given to Abraham might come to the Gentiles through Christ Jesus, so that by faith we might receive the promise of the Spirit"* (Galatians 3:14). That's pretty significant stuff! I am in the same cafeteria line with Abraham! I have a right to the same spiritual blessings on my tray as he had on his. And furthermore, I may not receive an exemption from pain or problems, but I have the "promise of the Spirit."

A pastor was talking to a group of young children about being Christians and going to Heaven. At the end of his talk, he asked, "Where do you want to go?"

"Heaven!" they all piped up.

Again, the pastor asked, "And what do you have to be to get there?"

"Dead!" one boy yelled.

We don't have to be dead to enjoy the blessings of Heaven. Some of them are ours here on earth—and we don't even have to live in West Virginia ("almost Heaven" as the commercial says) to enjoy them.

God is not limited by space or place! He is present everywhere, all the time. That's good news!

When I'm lonely, God's presence cheers me up.

When I'm uptight, God's presence calms me down.

When I'm troubled, God's presence helps me out.

When I'm discouraged, God's presence sees me through.

> *Where can I go from your Spirit? Where can I flee from your presence? If I go up to the heavens, you are there; if I make my bed in the depths, you are there. If I rise on the wings of the dawn, if I settle on the far side of the sea, even there your hand will guide me, your right hand will hold me fast. If I say, "Surely the darkness will hide me and the light become night around me," even the darkness will not be dark to you; the night will shine like the day, for darkness is as light to you.*

Psalm 139:7-12

GOD'S POWER

His power is awesome! And the amazing thing is that He wants to share it with you! But what good is God's power if you never experience it for yourself?

> *Do you not know? Have you not heard? The LORD is the everlasting God, the Creator of the ends of the earth. He will not grow tired or weary, and his understanding no one can fathom. He gives strength to the weary and*

increases the power of the weak. Even youths grow tired and weary, and young men stumble and fall; but those who hope in the LORD will renew their strength. They will soar on wings like eagles; they will run and not grow weary, they will walk and not be faint.

Isaiah 40:28-31

Living in Oklahoma, I think I've seen it all when it comes to tornadoes. I've seen wheat stubble driven through telephone poles. You might think, *How could such a flimsy substance as that be thrust through a rugged piece of wood?* The answer: only through its surrender to the awesome power of the tornado.

Even the weakest, the frailest—when surrendered to the awesome power of God—can do the impossible. As it says in Luke 18:27, *"What is impossible with men is possible with God."*

GOD'S PROVISION

The apostle Paul said in Philippians 4:19, *"My God will meet all your needs according to his glorious riches in Christ Jesus."* God has not promised to supply all of our greed. He has promised, however, to supply everything we need.

Many people try to meet their needs with uncertain, temporal things of this world. Take, for example, the lottery. We don't have a lottery in my home state of Oklahoma, but our Texas neighbors to the south do. Want to know what the odds are of winning the Texas Lotto jackpot? They are 25.8 million to 1. You have a better chance of being struck by lightning (3.4 million to 1). Shocking, isn't it? And yet people continue to shell out money for those tickets, week after week.

Trust in a certainty—God. He will take care of you (and all you have to do is ask).

GOD'S PROTECTION

Isaiah reminds us that *"He tends his flock like a shepherd: He gathers the lambs in his arms and carries them close to his heart; he gently leads those that have young"* (Isaiah 40:11).

I like the idea that the Lord is my shepherd. It makes me feel protected and cared for. How comforting! I do have to admit, however, that I'm not crazy about being compared to sheep. Sheep are dumb. They can't do tricks like my dog, Marmaduke. You never see sheep in a circus. Sheep are high-maintenance creatures. They tend to stray and get lost. Maybe the analogy fits better than one would expect. It's a good thing the Lord is our shepherd. We have need of nothing, and we can rest safe and secure in Him.

Deuteronomy 32:10-11 says, *"He shielded him and cared for him; he guarded him as the apple of his eye, like an eagle that stirs up its nest and hovers over its young, that spreads its wings to catch them and carries them on its pinions."*

GOD'S PEACE

We become uneasy when:

Predicaments are uncontrollable.

The ABC's of a Personal Relationship with Christ

Receiving Jesus Christ is as simple as ABC . . .

Admit that you have sinned.   Romans 3:23
Believe that Jesus Christ died for you.   John 1:12
Confess that Jesus Christ is Lord of your life.   Romans 10:9

"Dear Lord Jesus, I know that I am a sinner. I believe that You died for my sins and arose from the grave. I now turn from my sins and invite You to come into my heart and life. I receive You as my personal Savior and follow You as my Lord. Amen."

People are unchangeable.

Problems are unsolvable.

In John 14:27, our Lord gave reassuring words to His disciples, *"Peace I leave with you; my peace I give you. I do not give to you as the world gives. Do not let your hearts be troubled and do not be afraid."* Peace is not the absence of problems; peace is knowing that God is with us.

The peace God gives is not Pollyanna optimism that has its head in the clouds and refuses to see reality. Our peace rests in His abiding presence, looks life straight in the face, and says, "Go ahead—make my day!"

We can cope with the fragile times when we are secure in who we are: saved children of God.

2. WHOM SHALL I MARRY? (KNOWING THAT WE ARE NOT
    ALONE HELPS US TO COPE.)

As I did that turning-fifty reflection, I also thought about my years of marriage to Jimmy Carter's (not *that* Jimmy Carter) daughter, Linda, from South Georgia. When that preacher asked me if "I wilt," I'm sure glad "I wilted!" We have shared a mutual respect, friendship, and the kind of love that causes two people to stand with confidence against the winds of time. That Georgia peach has not only been my dearest traveling companion, she has been my dearest friend.

No wonder the apostle Paul gave this advice: *"Do not be yoked together with unbelievers. For what do righteousness and wickedness have in common? Or what fellowship can light have*

105

with darkness?" (2 Corinthians 6:14). The Stan and Linda team has endured some challenging overtimes and some faith-testing tenth innings, but we've also experienced great championships (including raising two wonderful sons).

Linda's bout with cancer caused us to realize how dependent we are on each other and how dependent we both are on our Lord. Indeed, part of the coping process is finding someone with whom to share the journey, especially someone who looks to the same Coach to guide the team through the rocky game of life.

When the going gets rough, I'm going with you!

It's great to have a best friend! Just like this couple:

Grandpa and Grandma were sitting in their porch rockers, watching the beautiful sunset and reminiscing about "the good old days," when Grandma turned to Grandpa and said, "Honey, do you remember when we first started dating and you used to just casually reach over and take my hand?"

Grandpa looked over at her, smiled, and took her aged hand in his.

With a wry little smile, Grandma pressed a little farther, "Honey, do you remember how, after we were engaged, you'd sometimes lean over and suddenly kiss me on the cheek?"

Grandpa leaned slowly toward Grandma and gave her a lingering kiss on her wrinkled cheek.

Growing bolder still, Grandma said, "Honey, do you remember how, after we were first married, you'd nibble on my ear?"

Grandpa slowly got up from his rocker and headed into the house. Alarmed, Grandma said, "Honey, where are you going?"

Grandpa replied, "To get my teeth!"

The affection and affirmation of our loved ones and friends are God's lifelines to us when we go through troubled waters. When we reflect on those trying times, we'll remember that we weren't alone.

3. WHAT SHALL I DO WITH MY LIFE? (LEARNING TO COPE MEANS DISCOVERING THE PURPOSE IN THE PAIN.)

Settling the issues of personal faith and choosing a Christian companion helped me learn how to cope with life, but settling on God's will for my life also gave me a great direction, one that was vital when the winds of adversity attempted to blow me off course.

Paul taught young Christians that there is an experience of surrender to the will of God that gives not only greater spiritual power but also spiritual purpose. *"May God himself, the God of peace, sanctify you through and through. May your whole spirit, soul and body be kept blameless at the coming of our Lord Jesus Christ. The one who calls you is faithful and he will do it"* (1 Thessalonians 5:23-24).

I heard about Aunt Lois who boarded an Amtrak train to Dallas from Oklahoma City. The conductor waited patiently as she searched through her purse, and then her pockets, for her ticket. Finally she said, "This is terrible! I know I had a ticket, but for the life of me I can't remember what I did with it."

The conductor said, "All is not lost, ma'am. You can pay me directly. Then when you find the ticket, you can return it and get your money back."

"But that's not the point," said Aunt Lois, bewildered. "I'm not worried about the money. I need that ticket to tell me where it is I'm going!"

Following my conversion to Christ, I hungered and thirsted for all God wanted me to be and all that He wanted me to do. I remember the time when I made the decision to fully consecrate my life to His purpose. At that moment, I knew where it was I was going—wherever God would lead.

That sense of purpose has helped me cope with the twists and turns of life. I knew that even if there was a bend in the road, I was heading the right way—that I would be led by the Conductor who not only knows my destination, but will travel with me every step of the way.

Happiness is not the end of life: character is.
—Henry Ward Beecher

WAITER, DOES THAT CORN ON THE COB COME WITH DENTURE ADHESIVE?

The closer I get to the senior side of the restaurant menu, the more I realize that the aging process has its own dangers and delights. The changing demographics are mind-boggling. Since 1900, the expected life span has increased from forty-seven years to seventy-six. In the United States alone, my baby-boomer generation is joining the "fabulous fifties" at a rate of ten thousand per day. We have redefined middle age—it's now fifty.

The numbers of folks who are staying home worrying will far outnumber those who are staying out late with the family car! Whether we fall into the "Boomer," "Builder," or "Bewildered" category, we all need a little help to cope with those buzzard-circlin' times.

Three elderly gentlemen were discussing their demise. The seventy-five-year-old said, "When I die, I hope it's in a hurry. I'd be satisfied to get hit by a shiny new sports car when I'm out jogging."

His eighty-five-year-old friend responded, "Not me. I'd like it to take a little more time. I'd like to skydive out of a plane, slowly pull the parachute cord, and float like a cloud for a good while. Then, if the parachute fails, I'd like to land in that field near the girls' dorm at that college down the road."

"Jake, how would you like to go?" his friends asked their ninety-year-old buddy.

Jake replied, "Well, boys, I'm hoping to die from smoke inhalation, blowing out 110 candles on my birthday cake!"

Now that's a coping attitude!

Coping with calamity begins in the mind. It begins with a determination to see it through to the end—and enjoy the journey in spite of it all.

Coping considers all the circumstances, places faith in God, and turns its back to the wind. Paul did just that. And at the end of his life, he gave an awesome testimony: *"I am*

already being poured out like a drink offering, and the time has come for my departure. I have fought the good fight, I have finished the race, I have kept the faith. Now there is in store for me the crown of righteousness, which the Lord, the righteous Judge, will award to me on that day—and not only to me, but also to all who have longed for his appearing" (2 Timothy 4:6-8).

I DON'T NEED A TORCH; MY HEARTBURN IS FIRE ENOUGH!

Like it or not, people around us are watching. They want to see us carry the torch, even in the rain. They want to know if there are "batteries included" in that faith of ours. They want to know if religion works when the opposition comes along.

A little boy ran to his mother, "Mom! You know that antique clock of ours that has been passed from one generation to another?"

"Yes," the mother anxiously responded. "What's wrong?"

"My generation just dropped it!"

Adversity or not, our generation cannot afford to drop the torch of faith. It must be passed along, not snuffed out by the circumstances we encounter.

Don't Take My Plate Just Yet, I'm Getting Up Enough Courage to Finish the Broccoli

(Surviving the Lean and Mean Times)

The famed New York Yankee catcher-philosopher Yogi Berra reminded the world, "It's not over 'til it's over." Coping never gets easier. Buzzard-circlin' times, like a roomful of preschoolers, will wear us out. We just have to decide we're going to make it to the end—whether we feel like or not.

Down in southern Ohio, Farmer Joe was involved in an accident. He decided his injuries from the accident were serious enough to take the trucking company responsible to court. In the courtroom, the trucking company's New York lawyer was questioning the farmer.

"Didn't you say you were fine at the scene of the accident?"

"S'pose I did," Joe responded. "But let me tell you what happened. I had just loaded my favorite mule Bessie into the . . . "

"I didn't ask for any details!" the lawyer loudly interrupted. "Just answer the question. At the scene of the accident, did you say, 'I'm fine'?"

Farmer Joe said, "Well, yes, but I'll tell you what happened. I had just loaded my favorite mule Bessie into the . . . "

The lawyer interrupted again and said, "Judge, I am trying to establish the fact that, at the scene of the accident, this man told the highway patrolman that he was just fine. Now, several weeks after the accident, he is trying to sue my client. I believe he is a fraud. Please tell him to simply answer the question."

By this time the judge was fairly interested in Joe's answer, and he said to the lawyer, "I'd like to hear what he has to say about his favorite mule Bessie."

The farmer thanked the judge and proceeded, "As I was saying, I had just loaded Bessie, my favorite mule, into the trailer and was driving her down the highway when this huge semi ran the stop sign and smacked my pickup truck right in the side. I was thrown into a ditch on one side of the road, and Bessie was thrown into a ditch on the other side.

"Judge, I was hurting real bad and didn't want to move. Lying there, I could hear ol' Bessie moaning and groaning. I just knew she was in terrible shape.

"Shortly after the accident, a highway patrolman did come on the scene. He heard Bessie, too, so he went over to her."

"What happened next?" the judge asked with interest.

"Your Honor, that patrolman came across the road with his gun in his hand and looked at me."

"And?" the judge asked, leaning forward on the bench.

Joe answered, "He said, 'Mister, your mule was in such bad shape, I had to shoot her.'" He continued, "Then, with the gun still in his hand and still smokin', that policeman looked at me and asked, 'And how are you feeling?'"

THAT TIMEX JUST KEEPS TICKING!

My father was killed in a tragic accident when I was eleven years old. Dad was a poor West Virginia coal miner. (If you've seen the movie *October Sky,* you can identify with my dad's life.)

In 1962, we moved to Ohio in search of a better life. Dad hired on as a construction worker and worked six months until he had the accident that took his life. My only inheritance was the Timex watch that he was wearing the day he was killed.

Every Monday morning I wind up the old watch, strap it on, and think about the lessons Dad taught me about life. Amazingly, the watch keeps perfect time and has never been serviced!

What were those lessons? I think they can be summed up in seven life principles:

Life Principle No. 1 No problem is too big for God's power, and no person is too small for God's love. *"God so loved the world that he gave his one and only Son, that whoever believes in him shall not perish but have eternal life"* (John 3:16).

Life Principle No. 2 A smile is the light in your face that tells everyone your heart is home. *"A cheerful heart is good medicine, but a crushed spirit dries up the bones"* (Proverbs 17:22).

Life Principle No. 3 God gave us two hands—one with which to receive and the other with which to give. *"Those who sow in tears will reap with songs of joy. He who goes out weeping, carrying seed to sow, will return with songs of joy, carrying sheaves with him"* (Psalm 126:5-6).

Life Principle No. 4 Life is like a ladder; every step we take is up or down. *"A simple man believes anything, but a prudent man gives thought to his steps"* (Proverbs 14:15).

Life Principle No. 5 An act of kindness, no matter how small, is never wasted. *"Whatever you do, whether in word or deed, do it all in the name of the Lord Jesus, giving thanks to God the Father through him"* (Colossians 3:17).

Life Principle No. 6 Music is the language of the soul. Stand on the tips of your toes when you sing! *"My heart is steadfast, O God; I will sing and make music with all my soul. Awake, harp and lyre! I will awaken the dawn. I will praise you, O LORD, among the nations; I will sing of you among the peoples. For great is your love, higher than the heavens; your faithfulness reaches to the skies. Be exalted, O God, above the heavens, and let your glory be over all the earth"* (Psalm 108:1-5).

Life Principle No. 7 The valley of the shadow of death holds no darkness for the child of God. *"Then I saw a new heaven and a new earth, for the first heaven and the first earth had passed away, and there was no longer any sea. I saw the Holy City, the new Jerusalem, coming down out of heaven from God, prepared as a bride beautifully dressed for her husband. And I heard a loud voice from the throne saying, 'Now the dwelling of God is with men, and he will live with them. They will be his people, and God himself will be with them and be their God'"* (Revelation 21:1-3).

I learned a great deal about living life from those fatherly nciples. And from his steadfast faith, I learned to keep ticking like that Timex, even when I've been beaten and battered by the events of earth. I graduated magna cum laude from the school of hard knocks. (My school colors were black and blue!)

A milestone birthday can cause one to reflect on the people who've been influential and the events that have shaped and formed one's life. When I hit my fiftieth birthday, I wrote out the five statements below. Following the model of the great apostle Paul, I renewed my commitment to finish the course and keep the faith:

1. I am committed to seeking God.

When it comes to seeking Him, we need to be as diligent as the saintly widow lady who lived next door to an atheist. Every day she prayed loud enough for the atheist to hear. The atheist thought, *This woman's crazy, praying all the time. Doesn't she know there isn't a God?*

Often, he would harass her. "You old fool, why do you waste your time praying? There is no God!" But she kept right on praying!

One day, she ran out of food. So she prayed, "God, I'm out of groceries. I need help today. By faith, I thank You in advance that the answer is already on the way!"

As usual, the atheist heard her praying and thought, *Here's an opportunity for me to prove to her there is no God.* So he went to the grocery store and bought a cartload of groceries, dropped them on her front porch, rang the doorbell, and hid by the side of her house to see what she would do. When she opened the door and saw the groceries, she started jumping up and down, praising her Lord.

The atheist jumped out from the side of her house and said, "There, now do you believe me? God didn't buy you those groceries—I bought them!" That just made her sing and shout all the more.

He said, "Didn't you hear me?"

She answered, "Yes, I did. I knew the Lord was gonna buy me some groceries, but I didn't know He was gonna have the devil pay for 'em!"

> *Not that I have already obtained all this, or have already been made perfect, but I press on to take hold of that for which Christ Jesus took hold of me. Brothers, I do not consider myself yet to have taken hold of it. But one thing I do: Forgetting what is behind and straining toward what is ahead, I press on toward the goal to win the prize for which God has called me heavenward in Christ Jesus.*

Philippians 3:12-14

2. I am committed to standing firm on my convictions.

On a British Airways flight from Johannesburg, South Africa, a middle-aged, well-off, white South African lady found herself seated next to a black man. She pushed the flight-attendant button to complain about her seating arrangements.

"What seems to be the problem, madam?" asked the attendant.

"Isn't it obvious? Can't you see this disgusting person seated next to me? Find me another seat. Immediately!"

"Calm down, madam," the flight attendant replied. "This is a full flight, but I'll see if by chance there's a seat in first class." The woman cocked a snooty look at the black man who dropped his head in despair.

Moments later, the flight attendant came back with good news. "Madam, we do have one available seat in first class." A self-satisfying grin came over her face. The flight attendant continued, "We don't usually make upgrades in seating, but given the circumstances, one should not be forced to sit next to an obnoxious person."

With that, the flight attendant turned to the black man sitting next to her and said, "Sir, if you would grab your bags, a seat in first class is now ready for you."

Now that's a flight attendant with conviction!

God "will give to each person according to what he has done." To those who by persistence in doing good seek glory, honor and immortality, he will give eternal life.

Romans 2:6-7

3. I am committed to my family.

I'm concerned about today's families. They are enjoying a higher standard of living than ever before—living in nicer houses—but our homes are in critical condition. Half of our marriages are failing. Divorce is bulldozing its way through our society.

Governor Frank Keating is passionate about saving marriages in Oklahoma. In fact, if you can prove that you have completed a premarital counseling course, you can get a marriage license at a discounted rate.

Not long ago a couple stopped by my office to inquire about our wedding services. I told them about my requirement for premarital counseling and the discount it would provide when they applied for a marriage license. The groom-to-be looked at me and said, "Marriage counseling? Why do I need marriage counseling? I've been married three times!"

> *The overseer must be above reproach, the husband of but one wife, temperate, self-controlled, respectable, hospitable, able to teach, not given to drunkenness, not violent but gentle, not quarrelsome, not a lover of money. He must manage his own family well and see that his children obey him with proper respect. (If anyone does not know how to manage his own family, how can he take care of God's church?)*

1 Timothy 3:2-5

4. I am committed to excellence in ministry.

Former president of the United States Jimmy Carter (from my wife's home state of Georgia) has always intrigued me. I once heard President Carter talk about his service in the Navy, graduating from Annapolis, and being interviewed by Admiral Rickover, who founded the U.S. Nuclear Navy. President Carter reminisced about Admiral Rickover's barrage of questions.

The admiral asked Carter, "Where did you stand in your graduating class at Annapolis?"

Jimmy Carter told him, "I wasn't at the top of the class, but I wasn't at the bottom of the class. I was kind of in the middle."

Ten Ways to Know if You're Ready for Children

1. Women: Put on a dressing gown and tie a beanbag chair around your waist. Leave it there for nine months. After nine months, remove 10 percent of the beans.

   Men: Go to the local drugstore and dump the contents of your wallet on the counter. Tell the pharmacists to help themselves. Then go to the supermarket and arrange to have your paycheck directly deposited into the store's account.

2. Find parents with children who misbehave and offer them advice about child rearing and discipline. Enjoy the experience. It will be the last time you'll have all the answers.

3. To discover how the nights will feel after you have a baby, set your alarm to go off every two hours between 10 P.M. and 5 A.M. Each time you get out of bed, carry around a wet bag weighing eight to twelve pounds. Sing songs and jiggle the bag. At 5 A.M., get up and make breakfast while trying to look cheerful. Keep this up for five years.

4. To anticipate the messes made by children, smear peanut butter and jelly on your sofa and curtains. Shove a mini pizza into your VCR. Take potting soil from your household plants and apply it directly to your wallpaper. Using crayons, draw hundreds of uneven circles on the lower part of your living-room walls. Now stand back and smile as you survey the scene.

5. To prepare for dressing small children, go to your local pet store and purchase a medium-sized octopus. Practice putting the octopus into a sandwich-sized zipper bag without any arms sticking out. Time allowed for this: all morning.

6. Trade in your two-door sports car for a minivan. Stick a chocolate ice cream bar in the glove compartment and leave it there all summer. Jam a quarter into the cassette player and smash a family-sized bag of chocolate cookies into the seats and grind them into the carpet with your heel. Then run a garden rake along the sides of the van. Now you have a "family vehicle."

7. Repeat everything you say at least five times—patiently.

8. Visit the local grocery store with the closest thing you can find to a preschool child. A full-grown goat is excellent. If you plan to have more than one child, take more than one goat. Buy your week's groceries without letting the goats out of your sight. Pay for everything the goats eat or destroy. Then herd the goats and groceries to your chocolate-stained minivan in the parking lot.

9. Hollow out a melon. Make a small hole in the side. Suspend it from the ceiling and swing it from side to side. Now take a bowl of soggy Fruit Loops and attempt to spoon them into the swaying melon by pretending to be an airplane. Continue until half the Fruit Loops are gone. Tip the rest into your lap, spilling a large amount on the floor. You're now ready to feed a small child.

10. Finally, think about the proudest moment in your life to date. Perhaps it was graduation or your wedding day or landing that important job. Add to that feeling the sensation you received when you first found out your husband or wife really loved you or when you made your parents proud or when someone looked up to you as a role model. Now multiply those combined feelings of exhilaration by one hundred, and add a broad smile and a chest-bursting sense of pride. If you can barely contain all that excitement and energy, you're ready to have children.[17]

The admiral then asked, "Did you do your best?"

Carter said, "I thought about it, and the only honest answer was—'No. I didn't do my best.'"

The admiral looked at him with piercing eyes and asked, "Why not? Why not the best?"

President Carter said, "That question was burned into my heart so much that it became a theme for my life, so that on every decision I'd ask myself, 'What's the best here?'"

"Keep your head in all situations, endure hardship, do the work of an evangelist, discharge all the duties of your ministry" (2 Timothy 4:5).

5. I am committed to maintaining an eternal perspective.

> *Do you not know that in a race all the runners run, but only one gets the prize? Run in such a way as to get the prize. Everyone who competes in the games goes into strict training. They do it to get a crown that will not last; but we do it to get a crown that will last forever. Therefore I do not run like a man running aimlessly; I do not fight like a man beating the air. No, I beat my body and make it my slave so that after I have preached to others, I myself will not be disqualified for the prize.*
>
> 1 Corinthians 9:24-27

I once heard of a grandpa who was well into his eighties before he decided to try a hearing aid. He was amazed at the fancy gadget's capabilities and stopped by to thank the audiologist who had assisted him. Grandpa told of his new ability to easily hear conversations, even in the next room. The hearing specialist was delighted. "Your relatives must be happy to know you can hear so well."

The wise elder replied with a smile, "Oh, I ain't told 'em. I've just been sittin' 'round the house listenin' to 'em. You know what? I've changed my will twice already."

I have determined not to change my will. I don't mean the legal document that gives everything I worked for to those I worked for in the first place. I mean, I am determined not to change my *will*, my inner resolve to meet the uncertainties of life with certain strength. With a dependence on the power and wisdom of a God who hasn't failed me, I am determined to cope with the calamities. And who knows, I may even take a sanctified swat at those buzzards circlin' overhead!

No matter what pitch life throws, whether it's a fastball or a curve, we can stand firm in the batter's box. We can cope— even to the very last. Why? Because for the child of God, the *very last* is just the beginning.

Awhile back an old friend, Glen Payne of Cathedral Quartet fame, passed away. Gospel singer Mark Lowry sent the following e-mail to me while Jim Hill, the writer of "What a Day That Will Be," happened to be in Oklahoma City, singing at my church.

Lowry wrote, "It's now Sunday night. I just got back from the funeral home. I saw Glen's wife, Van, [and] their children and their children's spouses. Van told me how Glen left this life. [Glen] would come in and out of consciousness and look wide-eyed toward the ceiling and around the room as if he were looking into eternity.

"Over and over again, Glen would say, 'Wow!' as he viewed the other side. But when he finally passed away, he was singing. Glen always said he wanted to go out of this life singing! Well, he did! He was singing, 'What a Day That Will Be.' When he got to the part, 'When He takes me by the hand, . . .' Glen took his last breath on this earth."

What a way to leave this world, singing about the place God has prepared for all of His children!

> *Our citizenship is in heaven. And we eagerly await a Savior from there, the Lord Jesus Christ, who, by the power that enables him to bring everything under his control, will transform our lowly bodies so that they will be like his glorious body.*

Philippians 3:20-21

Everything Isn't Relative; I've Also Got Some Good Friends

(Good Relationships Help Us through Tough Times)

Perhaps you've heard the story of the old Oklahoma philosopher who was sitting on his porch when a man and his family drove up in a frontier wagon. "Hey, mister!" the pioneer dad spoke up. "Is this here town friendly?"

"Depends," the philosopher replied. "How was the town where you came from?"

"Not at all friendly!" the pioneer announced. "That's why we left."

The wise old man responded, "Then you'll probably find this town to be the same way."

Later, an almost identical wagon filled with another pioneer family stopped and asked about the friendliness of the frontier town.

"How was it where you came from?" the philosopher asked.

"Friendliest town we ever saw!"

The old man said, "Probably find this town the same way."

Remember the advice we received as children: "If you want to have friends, you need to be friendly." Relationships take work. They aren't given out like political flyers. Relationships grow as a result of our efforts. And, most often, what we put into them is exactly what we get out of them. They take time, talent, tears, and treasure. But the payoff is worth the effort. When those relationships work, they can be a great source of encouragement and strength to see us through the buzzard-circlin' times.

This is seen in the life of Ruth, one of the great characters of the Bible. Born into a pagan culture, she found faith and family with the people of Israel. Her life story reads like the script of a daytime soap opera—minus immorality and commercials.

A man by the name of Elimelech (sounds like the lyrics to a fifties rock 'n' roll song) left his home country of Judah to find food. Famine had gripped his homeland, so Elimelech took his wife and two sons to Moab where there was plenty. Not long after settling in, tragedy struck the family. Elimelech died, leaving his wife, Naomi, to raise her young sons. The sons grew and married two women from Moab—Ruth and Orpah (not Oprah of talk-show fame).

Both of the sons died, and again Naomi was left. Her only comfort was the companionship of her daughters-in-law. Talk about buzzards circlin' overhead! Yet when the tough times roll in like a gray cloud, God has a way of recruiting personal "sunbeams" in the form of friends or loved ones.

Hearing that times were better in Judah, Naomi and her daughters-in-law headed back toward home. At one point in their journey, Naomi had a mother to daughter-in-law talk. In her wisdom, she encouraged her daughters-in-law to go back home. In essence, she said, "Look, I've run out of sons, and even if I gave birth to twins, you'd have a long wait before they could walk down the aisle!" Orpah grabbed the airline ticket and ran. But Ruth stayed. She was immediately inducted into the Daughter-in-law Hall of Fame.

WHAT'S A NICE GIRL LIKE YOU DOING IN A CRISIS LIKE THIS?

Naomi had probably packed sandwiches and a thermos for Ruth and Orpah's journey back to their homeland. Orpah took her sack lunch with her (she knew all she would get on the airplane was a package of birdseed and one-third of an orange juice can). Ruth turned down the lunch. The Bible records the beautiful scene:

> *Ruth replied, "Don't urge me to leave you or to turn back from you. Where you go I will go, and where you stay I will stay. Your people will be my people and your God my God. Where you die I will die, and there I will be buried. May the LORD deal with me, be it ever so severely, if anything but death separates you and me." When Naomi realized that Ruth was determined to go with her, she stopped urging her.*

Ruth 1:16-18

That's more than a convenient scripture passage for a wedding ceremony. It was a stellar act of commitment to someone who had faced very troubled times. Ruth traded the smooth jet flight to Moab for the rugged journey to Judah. She put her arm around her grieving mother-in-law and said, "I am with you." God often uses ordinary people for extraordinary assignments. Ruth knew that Naomi needed a friend more than she needed a daughter-in-law (and many mothers-in-law would agree). She traded the niceties of home for the uncertainties of the journey back to Judah and the life to follow.

131

When the duo reached their destination, they were the talk of the town (probably because they were such a sorry sight). They had traveled hundreds of miles. Their mascara was running. They hadn't done their nails in weeks.

"Hello, Naomi," her astonished friends greeted.

"Do not call me Naomi!" the weary traveler replied in Ruth 1:20. *"Call me Mara, because the Almighty has made my life very bitter."*

Certainly, the times were rough. She had endured about as much sorrow as a wife or mother could endure. But she had forgotten God's goodness in providing *that* friend. He had injected Heaven's compassion into the veins of a Moabite woman named Ruth, and it took! God's ambassador had been with Naomi every step of the way.

We've been there, haven't we? So caught up in our grief, we don't realize that God has provided someone to walk with us during desolate times. God wouldn't fail us. His ambassadors have been appointed to our "foreign countries." God often uses a good relationship to help us through bad times.

> *Success has nothing to do with what you gain in life*
> *or accomplish for yourself. It's what you do for others.*
> ## —Danny Thomas

PLEASE, DON'T HANG THAT SWEATER UP.

The news came as a shock. The beloved television neighbor Fred Rogers announced his retirement. Who would model relationships for us now?

Jesus clearly answered that question in Luke 10 in the story of the good Samaritan. The parable (story from life) in the Gospel of Luke focuses on relationships. It begins with a very important question. *"On one occasion an expert in the law stood up to test Jesus. 'Teacher,' he asked, 'what must I do to inherit eternal life?'"* (Luke 10: 25). This lawyer was probably quite good with questions, but he didn't grasp the full meaning of the issue.

A young boy also had a similar difficulty. In Sunday School, they were teaching the children how God had created everything, including human beings. Little Johnny seemed especially intent when they told him how Eve had been created out of one of Adam's ribs.

Later in the week his mother noticed him lying down as though he were ill, and she said, "Johnny, what is the matter?"

Little Johnny responded, "I can't go to school today, Mom."

"Why is that?" she asked.

Johnny groaned, "I have a pain in my side. I think I'm going to have a wife."

Johnny didn't quite get the full meaning of this Bible story, and neither did the lawyer in Jesus' parable. In fact, he was more concerned with trapping Jesus into making a politically incorrect statement than he was in learning about God's answer to his spiritual condition.

Still, his question was an important one. "Teacher, what must I do?" He thought he had the answer, just like a lot of folks. He thought he could work his way into the kingdom of God.

133

Jesus didn't bother to point out the contradiction in his question. You can't *do* something to *inherit* a gift. An inheritance is based on a relationship, not an achievement. As a matter of fact, Jesus didn't even answer the question. He simply turned the question around and directed him to the Scriptures as the basis of authority. *"What is written in the Law?"* (v. 26).

Quickly, the attorney quoted from memory, *"Love the LORD your God with all your heart and with all your soul and with all your strength"* (Deuteronomy 6:5).

The Master said, *"You have answered correctly. . . . Do this and you will live"* (Luke 10:28). But something in Jesus' manner put the lawyer on the defensive: *"He wanted to justify himself"* (v. 29). The lawyer used a diversionary tactic, asking another question: *"Who is my neighbor?"* (v. 29).

ACROSS THE FENCE, OR ACROSS THE TRACKS?

The lawyer was trying to wiggle out. He wanted to know if there was any room in the law for leaving someone out (i.e. Was it okay not to take everyone in?). "Where do I draw the line," he could well have asked, "across the fence or across the tracks?"

The rabbis had pondered these questions for centuries. Some said that your neighbor is your brother. Others taught that your neighbor is your fellow Israelite. Some of the religious teachers set even stricter limits.

People are still debating the question, and some of the answers are quite alarming. Dr. Billy Graham was asked what he considered to be the greatest social problem in the world.

He gave a one-word reply: "Racism." Excluding people because of their color, creed, or condition is still a tremendous problem in our society. Ruth was a "foreigner," but that didn't matter to Naomi. Naomi was from a different faith, but that didn't keep Ruth from making a commitment to her.

"Who *isn't* my neighbor," is the gist of the lawyer's inquiry. "Is there anyone I don't have to love?" The answer didn't come in the form of a sociology lecture but in the form of a story. Jesus pointed the man toward the Jericho Road.

Traveler muggings were almost a league sport in the first century. There was a seventeen-mile road that plunged 3,300 feet from the city of Jerusalem to the city of Jericho. Muggings and robberies were so frequent on that stretch of highway that it was called "the way of blood." Jesus' audience of one was all too familiar with that rugged road.

> *In reply Jesus said: "A man was going down from Jerusalem to Jericho, when he fell into the hands of robbers. They stripped him of his clothes, beat him and went away, leaving him half dead. A priest happened to be going down the same road, and when he saw the man, he passed by on the other side. So too, a Levite, when he came to the place and saw him, passed by on the other side. But a Samaritan, as he traveled, came where the man was; and when he saw him, he took pity on him. He went to him and bandaged his wounds, pouring on oil and wine. Then he put the man on his own donkey, took him to an inn and took care of him. The next day he took out two silver coins and gave them to the innkeeper. 'Look after*

him,' he said, 'and when I return, I will reimburse you for any extra expense you may have.'

"Which of these three do you think was a neighbor to the man who fell into the hands of robbers?"

The expert in the law replied, "The one who had mercy on him."

Jesus told him, "Go and do likewise."

Luke 10:30-37

The story has a twofold lesson. First, it's a great study of human nature. Second, it's a story rich in symbolism.

The reactions of those pedestrians on the Jericho Road make an interesting study of humanity. We see the humans we want to meet in our journeys and those whom we would aspire to be.

1. **The robbers cared only about themselves.** *"They stripped him of his clothes, beat him and went away, leaving him half-dead"* (v. 30). They typify the money-hungry, heartless criminal element. So what if they bring pain to the lives of others, as long as their selfish needs are met.

2. **The priest cared only about his religion.** *"When he saw the man, he passed by on the other side"* (v. 31). The priest in Jesus' parable couldn't stop. He was on his way to the temple. He had all the right college degrees, but he didn't have discernment. He had the Scriptures memorized, but he didn't practice them. By the way, people in trouble need more than our pious proclamations. They need religion with skin on it.

They need eyes and feet and hands that will see and go and reach down to help.

3. **The Levite cared only about his own.** *"When he came to the place and saw him, [he] passed by on the other side"* (v. 32). The Levite "saw," but he didn't have eyes for the man's wounds. He saw only the man's race and religion. *He's not one of us,* he most likely thought. *What would my people think if I associated with someone like him?*

4. **The Samaritan cared about others over himself.** *"When he saw him, he took pity on him. He went to him and bandaged his wounds, pouring on oil and wine. Then he put the man on his own donkey, took him to an inn and took care of him"* (vv. 33-34). It didn't matter who the wounded man was, where he came from, or where he was going. His clothes (or lack thereof) didn't matter. Only his calamity was important. This man needed help, and the Samaritan bridged the chasm that the others could not bridge for the sake of the wounded.

> *It's much easier to love humanity as a whole than to love one's neighbor.*
> —*Eric Hoffer*

EXCUSE ME, ISN'T THAT JESUS OVER THERE?

The second part of the lesson is its rich symbolism. The same Jesus who told the story is the one it so perfectly symbolizes. He taught us about redemptive relationships. *"Greater love has*

no one than this, that he lay down his life for his friends" (John 15:13). He taught us that compassion has no borders. *"Love the Lord your God with all your heart and with all your soul and with all your mind.' This is the first and greatest commandment. And the second is like it: 'Love your neighbor as yourself'"* (Matthew 22:37-39).

The wounded man is symbolic of a fallen race. He represents those people whom God loves who are victims of their own wrong direction. They're on the wrong road. And when the wounds of sin come, the solution is obvious. It isn't religion. It isn't education. It isn't organization. It's Jesus. *"The wages of sin is death, but the gift of God is eternal life in Christ Jesus our Lord"* (Romans 6:23).

A friend is one who walks in when others walk out.
—Walter Winchell

SECRET SERVICE SAMARITANS

Maybe there's a third lesson—the idea of help coming from a person, from a place we least expect. The hero of the parable in Luke is extremely unlikely, a Samaritan whom any respectable Israelite wouldn't associate with on a day-to-day basis. The principle is the same in the Old Testament account of Naomi and Ruth. Ruth was likely the last person Naomi would have expected support from. She was from the other side of the spiritual tracks. She was of a different nationality. Her claim to culture was probably a certificate from "Hooked on Phonics!" But her position in the problem was of royal importance. She was a "Secret Service Samaritan," an under-cover officer on assignment from Heaven.

And her compassion had an eternal effect. Later she met a kinsman of Naomi's and fell in love with him. His name was Boaz. His love for her reads like a romance novel (Ruth 2-4; read it and weep!). The offspring of their marriage was Obed, the father of King David in the lineage of the Messiah, the Lord Jesus Christ.

An Amish buggy driver cracked the whip at a horsefly buzzing over the horse's back. It expired immediately. His son was riding with him and said, "Nice shot, Father!"

Another horsefly hovered, and there was another crack of the whip. The results were the same.

Suddenly a wasp approached. The Amish man did nothing. "Father?" the boy wondered aloud, "why didst thou not crack thy whip?"

"Because, my son," the buggy driver said soberly, "he's got family nearby."[18]

We never know where our help will be coming from, but one thing's for sure: we've got family nearby. God has Secret Service Samaritans waiting behind every bush, building, or battlefront to step up and take our hand when the buzzards start circlin'. God won't fail us.

HERE'S THE CUP OF SUGAR I BORROWED.
WOULD YOU MIND MAKING ME SOME BROWNIES?

So, who is my neighbor? *"Which of these three do you think was a neighbor to the man who fell into the hands of robbers?"*

(Luke 10:36). The answer, of course, is anyone in need. If we've been *tended to* on the Jericho Roads of our lives, we have an obligation to be a *tend-er.* Loving people is a visible evidence of our love for God.

Who are those people? Well, often they are exactly the kind of folk you wouldn't want to be stranded on Survivor Island with! They include:

The taker—Always asking for something.

In one of my pastorates, I was able to lead a retired oil-field worker to the Lord. He was pretty rough around the edges but eager to work in the church. With his personality-a-plenty, I thought—*usher.* He would make a fine usher.

After several months of "ushing" (that's what ushers do, of course), I felt the old boy was ready to pray over the offering. When I called on him to pray, he used every cliché he'd heard other ushers use in their offertory prayers. However, as he closed, he got a little confused. He prayed, "Lord, bless the givers and the takers alike."

Maybe he wasn't too far off, for in life, there are givers and there are takers.

The drainer—Constantly pulling on our emotional strings.

The Bible says that we're to keep our distance from the drainers. *"In the name of the Lord Jesus Christ, we command you, brothers, to keep away from every brother who is idle and does not live according to the teaching you received from us"* (2 Thessalonians 3:6). Drainers are scorekeepers. They keep statistics on their relationships. "I did something nice for you last time; now it's your turn to do something nice for me."

My stepfather, Jack Hollingsworth, used to be in the trucking business. He often hauled steel out of Pennsylvania. When his trailer was full, the truck traveled quietly down the road. But when it was empty, it would bounce, rattle, and make all sorts of noise.

The drainers of life are like that. When they're on empty, they make an awful lot of noise until we load 'em up again.

The stifler—Intolerable and difficult.

The children of Israel were poised to cross over into the Land of Promise (Joshua 3). Twelve spies were sent over into Canaan to check out the prospects. Ten of the twelve were "stiflers." Joshua and Caleb were outnumbered by the stiflers. However, they did their best to convince Moses, Aaron, and all the people of Israel that it was "a land flowing with milk and honey." Joshua and Caleb were men of faith!

> **F**orward
>
> **A**ction
>
> **I**nspired
>
> **T**hrough
>
> **H**im

Faith always propels us. **Forward Action** is the evidence of our faith. **Inspired**—that's the motivation of our faith. **Through Him**—He's the power of our faith.

Don't let the stiflers of your life keep you wandering in the wilderness!

141

The sniper—They take aim at us daily. They're never pleased with anything, constantly putting us down.

The Bible reminds us not to hang out with snipers! *"Keep me, O LORD, from the hands of the wicked; protect me from men of violence who plan to trip my feet"* (Psalm 140:4).

The gossiper—Doesn't know when to shut-up.

I've heard my share of gossip. I used to hang out at my mother's beauty shops. Frequently, I would listen to people talking to each other while under the hair dryers. One day I heard a woman say, "I don't repeat gossip, so listen carefully." What a hoot!

Have you visited your doctor lately? What was the first thing he said? Of course, he said, "Stick out your tongue." Then he looked at it with a flashlight. Next, he put one of those tasty oversized Popsicle sticks on your tongue and said, "Say aaah." Then, he placed a thermometer under your tongue and took your temperature. Why all the attention to the tongue? The tongue reveals a lot of what's going on in the rest of the body.

No wonder the psalmist prayed, *"Set a guard over my mouth, O LORD; keep watch over the door of my lips"* (Psalm 141:3).

The pouter—Always whining.

Some people "rise and shine" in the mornings, while others "rise and whine." The pouter's favorite phrase is, "That's not fair—everybody else gets all the breaks."

I once heard about a guy who was so argumentative that he ate only food that disagreed with him. Be careful, I think he's still on the Survivor's Island!

God gives us relatives; thank God we can choose our friends!
—A. Mizner

Can we be friends to the drainers and whiners of life? Yes, we can, because we have a friend like Jesus! He is the greatest model of friendship the world has ever known. During His life on earth, He gave us three marvelous examples of a true friend.

1. **The Loving**—John 15:9, *"As the Father has loved me, so have I loved you. Now remain in my love."* He loves us without reservation. He loves us when we are right, and He loves us when we are wrong.

A monarch called his three daughters to him. "How much do you love your father?" he asked.

Two of the daughters replied that they loved him more than gold and silver.

"And how about you?" the king asked the third daughter.

She replied, "Father, I love you more than salt."

The answer didn't please the king. *Salt?* He thought, *What a strange remark.*

The cook of the royal household overheard the remark and was troubled by the king's response. The next morning, the king's breakfast was prepared without any seasoning. It was bland and tasteless. The king summoned the cook. "Why is my breakfast so tasteless?" he asked.

143

"There is no salt on it, your majesty," the cook replied.

His daughter's words came to mind. The king understood. His daughter loved him so much that nothing was good without him.[19]

2. **The Faithful**—Jesus says in Matthew 28:20, *"I am with you always, to the very end of the age."* Jesus is always by our side, a never-failing friend. He will never leave us alone!

When the great Presbyterian minister Donald Barnhouse's wife died, he was left with young daughters to raise alone. While driving to the funeral, which he conducted himself, he wanted to say something to explain all of this to his girls.

They stopped at a traffic light. It was a bright day, and the sun streamed into the car. A truck pulled up next to them and its shadow darkened the inside of the car. He turned to them and asked whether they would prefer to be hit by the truck or its shadow.

They answered, "The shadow can't hurt you."

He quoted Psalm 23:4, *"Even though I walk through the valley of the shadow of death, I will fear no evil, for you are with me."* Then he explained that their mother's death was as if she had been hit by a shadow. It was as if Jesus had stepped in the way in her place.[20]

3. **The Comforting**—In John 14:27 Jesus says, *"Peace I leave with you; my peace I give you. I do not give to you as the world gives. Do not let your hearts be troubled and do not be afraid."* After the death of his wife, North Carolina evangelist Vance Havner was inconsolable. In one of his last books, he described it like this:

I think of a year that started out so pleasantly for my beloved and me. We had made plans for delightful months ahead together. Instead, I sat by her bedside and watched her die of an unusual disease. She expected to be healed, but she died. Now, all hopes of a happy old age together are dashed to the ground. I plod alone with the other half of my life on the other side of death. My hand reaches for another hand now vanished, and I listen at night for the sound of a voice that is still. And I am tempted a thousand times to ask, "My God, why . . . ?"

But Havner ends his book with this paragraph:

You need never ask "Why?" because Calvary covers it all. When before the throne we stand in Him complete, all the riddles that puzzle us here will fall into place, and we shall know in fulfillment what we now believe in faith—that all things work together for good in His eternal purpose. No longer will we cry, "My God, why?" Instead, "alas" will become "alleluia," all question marks will be straightened into exclamation points, sorrow will change to singing, and pain will be lost in praise.[21]

I'll never forget the day my father died. My Uncle Roy picked us up in Dad's old '59 Plymouth after school and said, "We need to go to the hospital. Your dad has been hurt in an accident."

Uncle Roy drove us to Doctor's North Hospital in Columbus, Ohio. My younger brothers and I waited in the car for about five hours while Mom shuttled in and out of the hospital. Finally a policeman came out and told us our dad had passed away.

When we got home, I didn't even want to get out of the car and go into the house. My heart pounded in despair as my brothers—Terry, age nine, and Mark, age three—sobbed and clung to me in the backseat of the car. Mother was so distraught that Uncle Roy had to help her into the house.

With my brothers' arms wrapped around me, I started up the steps; but I could go no farther. Gut-wrenching agony overtook me. I collapsed and wailed in pain. I felt as if I were lost, completely lost, on a sea of suffering. Confusion hurled itself upon me. I felt desperate. My eleven-year-old mind couldn't fathom how this could be. It simply didn't make sense. I wanted to run and hide. I didn't believe I could face the pain I was feeling. Hysterically I cried out, "Oh, God—I can't go into the house again without my daddy!"

Then I heard an almost audible voice—God's voice: "Yea, though I walk through the valley of the shadow of death. . . ." Immediately I felt the assurance that I was not alone—the Lord was with me. I stood up, wiped my eyes, and walked into the house on my own. An amazing peace swept over my soul, a peace that gave me the courage to face the difficult days to come.[22]

4. **The Consoler**—Matthew 9:36: *"When he saw the crowds, he had compassion on them, because they were harassed and helpless, like sheep without a shepherd."*

In 1996, contemporary Christian singer/songwriter Cindy Morgan arrived for a series of concerts in Los Angeles. As she unpacked her clothes for that evening's concert, she discov-

ered her dress was terribly wrinkled. One of the women helping with the concert set out to find an iron. She was sent to a
staff member's house with a key and instructions as to where
she would find the ironing board. To her horror, she entered
the house only to find the teenage daughter was home with a
loaded gun. She had been about to commit suicide when the
woman arrived. Through quick thinking, a cool head, and the
presence of God, she was able to talk the troubled teen into
dropping the gun and returning with her for help. In response
to God's miraculous intervention, Cindy Morgan said, "To
rescue a life, He wrinkled a dress."[23]

5. **The Helpful**—Mark 1:31: *"He went to her, took her
hand and helped her up. The fever left her and she began to
wait on them."*

A father was trying to explain the creation to his son as
they walked through the woods. "Son, God made all of this—
every single leaf on every single tree."

"Yes, I know, Dad," the boy responded excitedly, "and He
did it all with His left hand!"

"With His left hand?" the father asked. "Where did you
ever hear that?"

"Last week, my Sunday School teacher read from the Bible,
and it said that Jesus was sitting on His Father's right hand."

Our friendship is simply an extension of our relationship
with God. He is its source. He is its supply. He is its correc-
tion. He is its duration. Everything necessary to befriend a
person in need comes from Him. *"I am the vine; you are the*

branches. If a man remains in me and I in him, he will bear much fruit; apart from me you can do nothing" (John 15:5).

> *The best time to make friends is before you need them.*
> —*Ethel Barrymore*

The characteristics of our friendship arise from our character. Mother Teresa exemplified some of the same characteristics as Ruth of the Old Testament. Her tenacious love for the unloved, her unwavering loyalty to the cause of helping them out of their plight, and her outstanding courage in defending their weakness are characteristics seen in Ruth's commitment to her family. Teresa, the saintly servant to the outcast of India, paraphrased the instructions of our Lord (Matthew 25), and gave us an interesting job description for being a neighbor:

My Neighbor

When I was hungry, you gave me to eat.
When I was thirsty, you gave me to drink.
When I was weary, you helped me find rest.
When I was anxious, you calmed all my fears.
When I was little, you taught me to read.
When I was lonely, you gave me your love.
When I was on a sick bed, you cared for my needs.
In a strange country, you made me at home.
Hurt in a battle, you bound up my wounds.
Searching for kindness, you held out your hand.[24]

> —*Mother Teresa*

KINDNESS IN A CUP OF COFFEE

Sharing.

Caring.

Loving.

Sacrificing.

These are actions of our friends and loved ones that have helped to lighten our load when the buzzards were dive-bombing the battlefields of our lives. So, we use those same actions to reach out to others. If we've borrowed a cup of sugar from someone in our time of need, then we ought to do more than ask for brownies. We ought to do some baking ourselves!

Several years ago while speaking on the same program with the late Dr. Charles Allen, I heard him tell a heartwarming story about Sam Rayburn, Speaker of the United States House of Representatives, who served in that position longer than any other man in our history. This story reveals the kind of man he was:

> One night, the teenage daughter of a friend of Speaker Rayburn died suddenly. Early the next morning the grieving father heard a knock at his door. When he opened it, there was Speaker Rayburn.
>
> Rayburn said, "I just came by to see what I could do to help."
>
> The father replied, "I don't think there is anything you can do, Mr. Speaker. We are making all the arrangements."

"Well," Mr. Rayburn said, "have you had your coffee this morning?"

The man replied that the family had not taken time for breakfast. So Mr. Rayburn said that he could at least make coffee for them. While he was working in the kitchen, the father came in and said, "Mr. Speaker, I thought you were supposed to be having breakfast at the White House this morning."

"Well, I was," Mr. Rayburn said, "but I called the president and told him I had a friend who was in trouble, and I couldn't come."[25]

Just think of those coffee cups filled with kindness. We've had more of them than we realize. Whether they were straight-up decaf or some Colombian mix, each had enough of a jolt to keep us going when the going was rough.

Flowers delivered to our house.

A pie.

An offer to baby-sit.

A phone call.

A greeting card.

Volunteering to mow our lawn.

A drive to the doctor's office.

Just random acts of kindness? Probably not. More likely, they were acts of care instituted by God and inspired in the heart of a friend. God will not fail us when the floods come. His mercy is everlasting—along with His everlasting friendship!

If you could choose one characteristic that would get you through life, choose a sense of humor.
—Jennifer Jones

Help, I've Fallen, and I Don't Want to Get Up

(Settling the Issues That Hinder Healing)

I t started off as an unbelievable e-mail, but the story which circulated, about shooting dead chickens through windshields, is true. NASA developed a gun to launch dead chickens 19,000 mph at windshields of space shuttles to test the shields' strength. Britain borrowed the gun to test it on their high-speed trains. When they fired it, the chicken smashed the windshield, ripped off the engineer's backrest, and embedded itself in the back wall of the cabin.

The British went to the Americans and asked, "What went wrong?"

The American scientists simply replied, "Thaw the chicken."

NASA spokesman Mike Braukus confirmed that the story is indeed true. He said, "That happened a year ago [1999]."

We all know the drill, "When all else fails, read the directions." With God's Word, we demonstrate wisdom by reading the directions first so "all else" won't fail.[26]

Sometimes we fail, and we don't want to get up. "Who cares about directions?" we ask.

Have you ever had a family of giraffes over for dinner? Neither have I, but I can only imagine what an evening like that might be like. First, my wife would be scurrying around trying to find a recipe for a "hay casserole." Second, we'd have to put duct tape around the chandelier in the dining room.

(It's expensive, and you know what a beating it would take every time those giraffes nodded yes to one of my questions!) Then, we'd have to position the crystal water glasses on the floor underneath the table because giraffes are used to stooping down to take a drink.

The dining-room chairs would have to be wired for reinforcement.

We'd have to put a tarp over the houseplants so they wouldn't be eaten as appetizers.

And you can only imagine how much fun it would be to do the cleaning-up after the guests have finally gone home!

The more I think about it, I bet the best thing about having a family of giraffes over for dinner would be the goodbyes at the door!

Unresolved issues in our hearts are like a family of giraffes. When we entertain them, they're awkward. They wreak havoc with our routines. They make us do or say things we wouldn't normally do or say. And they make the buzzard-circlin' times of our lives even more difficult.

The best part about dealing with them is telling them goodbye!

My friend Jerry Brecheisen says one of his least favorite ads is the one that boasts, "Learn to play the piano by ear." He says it's an advertising oxymoron. If you have an "ear" for music, you have a *natural* ability to hear the music pitch, memorize a tune, and then be able to sing or play it without having the notes in front of you. He says trying to teach a natural skill is like "teaching a seal to swim with a life preserver."

The apostle Peter played life by ear—naturally.

Reading his life story, one will find that he wasn't restricted to playing the notes. Called to be a disciple of Christ from a career as a commercial fisherman, he is one of the most interesting characters in the Bible. At times, his off-the-cuff actions and reactions looked like a script from the *Jerry Springer Show*.

One of his claims to fame was the time he took a sword and played Zorro on the ear of a government bureaucrat. You remember the night when Jesus was taken prisoner on the trumped-up charges of the government and the religious hierarchy. Peter was so enraged by the injustice, he took matters into his own hands. John 18:10 says: *"Simon Peter, who had a sword, drew it and struck the high priest's servant, cutting off his right ear."*

Jesus called John and his brother James the *"Sons of Thunder"* (Mark 3:17). And rightfully so! If there was a storm around, Peter was either waving his fist at the clouds or walking on the waves! He was one of the most courageous—and often outrageous—disciples on Jesus' winning team.

The apostle Peter was a tenderhearted servant of the Master. You remember the sadness of his heart over the crucifixion of Jesus was replaced with an overwhelming joy at the news of the resurrection. Peter won the hundred-yard dash to the empty tomb and left the other disciples eating dust.

I guess you could say Peter was like a test driver for a roller-coaster company. From time to time he struggled with some issues in his heart that resulted in some spiritual highs and lows. We've been on the same ride! Unresolved issues have hindered the healing flow in our hearts when the buzzards were circlin' overhead—especially when we have refused to deal with them. We have learned that they must be resolved if we are to gain victory.

What are some of those issues? Let's review several (not necessarily in any order of priority).

1. The Forgiveness Issue

Peter's intensity often brought him into conflict with those around him. Though he later became a great leader in the first-century church, he struggled early on to meet the demands of discipleship, including working with people. One day, Jesus gave a stirring lesson on the principles of reconciliation.

> *If a man owns a hundred sheep, and one of them wanders away, will he not leave the ninety-nine on the hills and go to look for the one that wandered off? And if he finds it, I tell you the truth, he is happier about that one sheep than about the ninety-nine that did not wander off. In the same way your Father in heaven is not willing that any of these little ones should be lost.*
>
> *If your brother sins against you, go and show him his fault, just between the two of you. If he listens to you, you have won your brother over. But if he will not listen, take one or two others along, so that "every matter may be established by the testimony of two or three witnesses." If he refuses to listen to them, tell it to the church; and if he refuses to listen even to the church, treat him as you would a pagan or a tax collector.*

I tell you the truth, whatever you bind on earth will be bound in heaven, and whatever you loose on earth will be loosed in heaven.

Matthew 18:12-18

The Master emphasized that forgiveness should be taken to its highest level—giving the accused every opportunity to be reconciled to the accuser.

Afterward, Peter approached Jesus with a question that reflected the deepest concerns of his heart. It very well could have been that Peter was concerned about a friendship that had "gone south." *"Lord, how many times shall I forgive my brother when he sins against me? Up to seven times?"* (Matthew 18:21). Forgive seven times? This was a magnanimous gesture on Peter's part. At that time it was generally understood that if you had suffered with a friend through three challenges to a relationship, you had done all you could reasonably be expected to do.

Jesus' response gives us a clear commentary on dealing with forgiveness issues. *"I tell you, not seven times, but seventy-seven times"* (v. 22). Peter asked if there were limits. The definitive answer was, "Absolutely not." Four hundred ninety times for every offense, and then the cycle of forgiveness repeats itself. No "hanging chads" here!

Not long ago, my golfing pal Huston Hall brought me a tape of Adolph Coors' personal testimony. Coors grew up in the Colorado mountains where his father built the Coors Brewing Company into a family fortune.

Adolph related the story of his father's driving to the brewery from their snowy mountain home one day when he saw a stranded motorist and pulled over to the side of the road. Unwittingly, Coors had walked into a deadly trap. The supposed stranded traveler was, in fact, a murderous kidnapper. He killed Adolph's father and attempted to extort money from the family through a ransom note. But his plot was discovered, and he eventually went to prison.

Adolph confessed that this childhood event caused so much bitterness and hatred that it tainted his adult life. Coors testified that as his marriage, career, and family crumbled around him, he sought forgiveness through the shed blood of Jesus Christ. Coors, who became a Christian, began to put Ephesians 4 into practice. Ultimately, Adolph Coors went to the prison cell that held his father's murderer and forgave him. What relief he experienced through this difficult experience![27]

To err is human, but when the eraser wears out
ahead of the pencil, you're overdoing it.
—*J. Jenkins*

2. The Resentment Issue

An unforgiving spirit is a hindrance to our spiritual and emotional healing. I love to tell the story of the little boy who was sitting on his front porch enjoying his candy bar when one of his friends stopped by. The boy placed his candy bar on the porch railing and went inside to answer a question that his mother had hollered through the screen door.

The temptation was too great. The friend grabbed the candy bar (which was his favorite) and ran like a beagle in a field full of rabbits. When the little boy returned to the porch, he noticed that both the candy bar and the friend had vanished. Soon the pursuit was on—the friend running down the street eating the candy bar, and the boy with a candy-bar-sized grudge chasing him.

The midair tackle was accomplished right in front of the boy's church. After the tackle, the little boy sat on his friend's chest and got nose to nose with the villain. Out of the corner of his eye, he saw the pastor coming out of the church's front door. He exclaimed loud enough for the pastor to hear, "Of course, I'll *forgive*, but it would be easier to *forget* it if you'd taken the time to wipe that candy bar off your face!"

His fake forgiveness didn't exactly qualify him for a spot on one of those stained-glass windows in a quaint European cathedral. A saint he ain't!

His "forgiver" was in pretty good shape, but his "forgetter" needed to be taken to the shop for repairs! The problem was, the evidence was still around. And as long as there was candy-bar residue on his friend's face, the issue was still alive.

Know anyone with a candy bar on his or her face? Are there issues of resentment that you can't resolve because the evidence is still around?

"How many times, Lord? Seven?"

"That's a good start, but guess again."

The seeds of healing won't grow in a heart of stone. To forgive means to "give up" or "to release." Jesus taught Peter that mercy and love are at the core of genuine forgiveness.

Neil Anderson said, "We must forgive in the same way we have been forgiven. In His mercy, God has given us what we need, not what we deserve."

If you know someone who has your "candy bar" on his or her face, let him go:

> the one who broke up your marriage,
>
> the one who abused you as a child,
>
> the people who wounded you in a church split,
>
> the one who took advantage of you,
>
> the one who neglected you.

Release feelings of resentment. It's the only way you'll find healing. Jesus said it, and I believe it: *"When you stand praying, if you hold anything against anyone, forgive him, so that your Father in heaven may forgive you your sin"* (Mark 11:25).

Never does the human soul appear so strong and noble as when it foregoes revenge and dares to forgive an injury.
—E.H. Chapin

3. The Anger Issue

A father was pushing a stroller through a city park. The baby was screaming at the top of his lungs. It was a summer day, and the park was filled with people, all watching.

As the embarrassed young man passed by, he was saying, "Take it easy, Fred, just relax. No reason to get excited. Just calm down, and everything will be all right. Come on, Fred. Just trust the Lord."

An older lady drew alongside and said, "My, what a nice baby. Did you say his name is Fred?"

"No, ma'am," said the father. "His name is John—my name is Fred!"

Anger is an issue that must be dealt with if we're going to experience any relief during our buzzard-circlin' times. It's like a pair of muddy boots on a new carpet. It's heavy. It's messy. And the further it goes, the more enemies it makes. Sometimes our anger isn't so obvious. Sometimes it just blossoms like a dandelion weed on a new lawn.

"I deserved that raise. I worked harder than he did, and all I have to show for it is poor health."

"They leased another new car? If it weren't for these legal bills, we could drive a nice car too!"

"How can she afford to dress like that? She doesn't know what it is to suddenly be a single mom and to support a family."

"They're expecting a child? We've always wanted children."

"He calls himself a Christian? Did you see the way he treated me?"

The accomplishments, accumulations, and actions of others make our own setbacks and losses more difficult to bear. And if we dwell on them, they become festering sores over our anger.

Jesse Jackson once told the story about his visit with the late Senator Hubert Humphrey just three days before Mr. Humphrey died. Humphrey had just called Richard Nixon, and many people wondered why. They had been longtime opponents, both politically and philosophically. Sometimes the differences had been bitter. When Jackson asked Senator

Humphrey why he had made such a call, Humphrey answered, "Jesse, from this vantage point, with the sun setting in my life, all of the speeches, the political conventions, the crowds, and the great fights are behind me now. At a time like this you are forced to deal with your irreducible essence, forced to grapple with that which is really important to you. And what I have concluded about life—when all is said and done, we must forgive each other, and redeem each other, and move on."[28]

The apostle Paul said, *"Get rid of all bitterness, rage and anger, brawling and slander, along with every form of malice. Be kind and compassionate to one another, forgiving each other, just as in Christ God forgave you"* (Ephesians 4:31-32).

4. The Doubt Issue

Another roller-coaster incident in Peter's life took place on the Sea of Galilee. Jesus had just performed the miracle of feeding five thousand people with five loaves and two fishes:

> *Immediately Jesus made the disciples get into the boat and go on ahead of him to the other side, while he dismissed the crowd. After he had dismissed them, he went up on a mountainside by himself to pray. When evening came, he was there alone, but the boat was already a considerable distance from land, buffeted by the waves because the wind was against it.*
>
> *During the fourth watch of the night Jesus went out to them, walking on the lake. When the disciples saw him*

*walking on the lake, they were terrified. "It's a ghost,"
they said, and cried out in fear.*

*But Jesus immediately said to them: "Take courage!
It is I. Don't be afraid."*

*"Lord, if it's you," Peter replied, "tell me to come to
you on the water."*

"Come," he said.

*Then Peter got down out of the boat, walked on the
water and came toward Jesus. But when he saw the
wind, he was afraid and, beginning to sink, cried out,
"Lord, save me!"*

*Immediately Jesus reached out his hand and caught
him. "You of little faith," he said, "why did you doubt?"
And when they climbed into the boat, the wind died down.*

*Then those who were in the boat worshiped him, say-
ing, "Truly you are the Son of God."*

Matthew 14:22-33

The incident is an interesting study in trusting the Lord
during the storms.

The worst of times come even to the best of folk. The
disciples were on this little *Titanic*. It wasn't a bunch of drug
runners. It wasn't a boatload of smugglers. It was God's
team. None of us are exempt from a little "boat tossing"
once in a while.

*Give me a sense of humor, Lord;
Give me the grace to see a joke,*

To get some happiness from life
And pass it on to other folk.
—Anonymous

Jesus was watching the boat. Nobody in that boat had to dial 911 on his cell phone. By the time the waves started doing their thing, the Master was already doing His! He may be silent in some of our storms, but He is never inactive!

Humor is the lifeboat we use on life's river.
—Anonymous

The fear of the unknown is the forerunner of doubt. The spiritual paralysis of the disciples began with their uncertainty about who was in control of the situation: ghost or God? This was a new experience, to say the least. They not only hadn't been in a storm like this before, they hadn't seen God reveal Himself like this. We'll never be able to trust the Lord in our traumas as long as we're trying to figure out how He's gonna get us out!

Peter wasn't listening. The apostle was so wrapped up in the incident, he didn't hear the most important words: "It is I. Don't be afraid." In the days of "CB Mania," when it seemed like everyone had a citizen's-band radio and a handle, one of the key broadcast phrases was, "Hey, good buddy, got your ears on?" Translated that means, "Hey, stupid, are you listening to your radio?" The dimmer one probably was the questioner, not the questionee, because if the radio wasn't on, how would the question be heard in the first place? The apostle Peter didn't "have his ears on." He wasn't tuned in to the presence of the Lord in the midst of the storm. Otherwise, He would have heard His voice.

Peter was all right as long as he kept his eyes on Jesus. That oft-taught principle is usually the first thing that is overlooked when the storms come. Perhaps we ought to say it to ourselves every day, many times a day: "Jesus first, storms second."

Peter's faith was pitiful (but it sure beat the faith of the ones in the boat). A little faith is better then none at all. If all we can muster is a little bit of trust when the buzzards start circlin', then let's go for it! Trust the Lord for an hour if you can't trust Him for a day. Trust Him to take care of the little, if you can't trust Him for a lot. Faith breeds faith!

We have to deal with the issue of doubt. James the apostle wrote, *"If any of you lacks wisdom, he should ask God, who gives generously to all without finding fault, and it will be given to him. But when he asks, he must believe and not doubt, because he who doubts is like a wave of the sea, blown and tossed by the wind"* (James 1:5-6).

Doubt does several things. First, it stops the flow of grace. James refers to a "God who gives generously." When we tape question marks over the pipeline of Heaven, it stops the flow of God's resource for our time of need. Second, it makes an unstable situation even more so, like the waves of the sea at the mercy of the wind. In the very beginning, doubt facilitated chaos. Eve rehearsed the warning God gave not to eat from the tree of the knowledge of good and evil. The devil questioned the order: *"'You will not surely die,' the serpent said*

to the woman. 'For God knows that when you eat of it your eyes will be opened, and you will be like God, knowing good and evil'" (Genesis 3:4-5).

Third, doubt causes us to play God. As we've seen, doubt is a way for us to try and take control of the buzzard-circlin' situation. "If God can't, then maybe I'll give it a try."

The Bible speaks of a time when all tears shall be wiped away. But it makes no mention of a time when we shall cease to smile.
—J.D. Eppinga

5. The Pain Issue

It's far easier to write books about dealing with pain than it is to deal with it personally. When it comes to suffering, I'd rather be in the stands cheering others on than to be out on the playing field! Pain, emotional or otherwise, is a relentless enemy that seeks to break down the very last strongholds of our mind, body, or spirit. Peter wrote about the devil's destructive delights, saying, *"Be self-controlled and alert. Your enemy the devil prowls around like a roaring lion looking for someone to devour. Resist him, standing firm in the faith, because you know that your brothers throughout the world are undergoing the same kind of sufferings"* (1 Peter 5:8-9).

Buzzards love to circle over the suffering. Usually they're not just observing, they're saying grace! While we're praying, "Now I lay me down to sleep. . . ." they're praying, "God is great and God is good, let us thank Him for our food!" They don't have a clue, however, that in this moment of misery, God isn't their food source.

No matter where it comes from, we have to learn how to deal with pain. Notice what happened when members of Peter's family were touched by suffering. Jesus was teaching in the Jewish synagogue when He received word that Peter's relative was ill. Notice the response, *"Jesus left the synagogue and went to the home of Simon. Now Simon's mother-in-law was suffering from a high fever, and they asked Jesus to help her"* (Luke 4:38).

As important as His teaching assignment was, Jesus responded to the cry of the suffering. That's the first clue in dealing with pain: Jesus is always on call. Give it to Jesus. Ask for His help. Call for Him even before you call for outside help. The psalmist David learned that secret of relying on the Lord in times of difficulty. Psalm 86:7 says, *"In the day of my trouble I will call to you, for you will answer me."*

Secondly, realize that pain is normally only temporary. I like the classic story of the government inspector who went into a blacksmith shop. The blacksmith warned the inspector not to touch a horseshoe that had just been taken out of the fire. Human nature kicked in, and the bureaucrat had to see for himself whether the blacksmith's word was true. He gently touched the orange-glowing horseshoe and jerked his hand back very quickly. "Burned ya, didn't it?" The smith inquired.

The government inspector held his throbbing fingers and replied, "No, it just doesn't take me that long to inspect a horseshoe!"

The last page of the Book is the last word on pain. Revelation 21:4 says, *"He will wipe every tear from their eyes. There will be no more death or mourning or crying or pain, for*

the old order of things has passed away." Our pain on earth will only last for a while, but our healing in Heaven will last forever.

I don't propose to be able to answer all the difficult questions about particular situations. Life is too complex, at least for me. But I do know that if we settle some issues, our hearts will be more settled.

I look to Jesus as the only worthy model, and I see that:

He loved a world that hated Him.

He stretched out His hands to those who would pierce Him with nails and didn't resent them.

He walked the dusty roads of life preaching a message of good news to those who doubted Him.

He blessed people who cursed Him.

When they wounded Him, He prayed, "Father, forgive them."

Peter had a lot of issues to settle, but Peter settled a lot of issues! As a matter of fact, Peter was the only disciple restored personally by Jesus. John 21:15-19 says:

When they had finished eating, Jesus said to Simon Peter, "Simon son of John, do you truly love me more than these?"

"Yes, Lord," he said, "you know that I love you."

Jesus said, "Feed my lambs." Again Jesus said, "Simon son of John, do you truly love me?"

He answered, "Yes, Lord, you know that I love you."

Jesus said, "Take care of my sheep." The third time he said to him, "Simon son of John, do you love me?"

Peter was hurt because Jesus asked him the third time, "Do you love me?"

He said, "Lord, you know all things; you know that I love you."

Jesus said, "Feed my sheep. I tell you the truth, when you were younger you dressed yourself and went where you wanted; but when you are old you will stretch out your hands, and someone else will dress you and lead you where you do not want to go." Jesus said this to indicate the kind of death by which Peter would glorify God. Then he said to him, "Follow me!"

Three times he messed up. Three times he 'fessed up. And three times, the mercy and grace of Christ touched his life.

Peter trusted Jesus enough during his lifetime that he could trust Him when it came time to die. Peter died a martyr's death. But I believe even then, in his heart, he was walking across the storms toward the Prince of Peace.

Now it's your turn.

This is the testimony: God has given us eternal life, and this life is in his Son. He who has the Son has life; he who does not have the Son of God does not have life.

1 John 5:11-12

I Know I'm Lost, but the Scenery's Spectacular!

(Finding the Purpose in the Problem)

While driving in a remote camping area, the father of a vacationing family came across a large sign that read, "Road Closed. Do Not Enter." The man proceeded around the sign because he was confident it would save them time on their journey. His wife was resistant to the adventure, but there was no turning back for this persistent road warrior. After a few miles of successful navigation, he began to boast about his gift of discernment.

His proud smile was quickly replaced with humble sweat when the road led to a washed-out bridge. He turned the car around and retraced his tracks to the main road. When they arrived at the original warning sign, his wife and three children all read the hand-painted message out loud—in unison, "Welcome back, stupid!"[29]

About the time we think we've got the route all figured out, along comes a dead end or a washed-out bridge that tries our spirit to the very limit. It may be a disease, a natural disaster, a financial setback, a broken relationship, or some other calamity, but its effects are quite common. What happens next means the difference between spiritual victory or spiritual defeat.

The natural man looks to the gray skies and sees the buzzards of doubt flying overhead like a squadron of Word War II jet fighters at an air show. Then double doubt kicks in. We question God. "What did I do to deserve this?" If that isn't bad enough, the devil sets up an unholy campsite on our shoulders and spends the night singing campfire songs of mockery and unbelief. "He's failed you, hasn't He?" the enemy croons. "God said He would take care of you, but just look at yourself!"

Suddenly it's "Wrestlemania!" We're in the ring bouncing between the problems and the promises. Paul describes us as *"infants, tossed back and forth by the waves, and blown here and there by every wind of teaching and by the cunning and craftiness of men in their deceitful scheming"* (Ephesians 4:14).

But there's another way—a better way. It's not a way of doubt, rather it's a way of discovery. It's making a concerted effort to discover God's purpose in the problems of life. Though we'll never fully understand His ways, as Isaiah the prophet reminds, *"Who has understood the mind of the LORD, or instructed him as his counselor?"* (Isaiah 40:13), God allows us to make just enough of a discovery about His will that it will give us enough strength for our storms.

Speaking of storms, there was a man in the Bible who was so familiar with them, we could set our navigational sights by simply pointing to him. His name is Jonah—you know, the "whale guy." His story gives us a wonderful insight into discovering purpose in the pains of our lives.

FISH AND A CHIP ON THE SHOULDER

People naturally associate the Old Testament character Jonah with a whale. Yet Jonah didn't spend his whole life

Top Ten Things People Won't Say When They See a Christian Bumper Sticker on Your Car

10. "Look! Let's stop that car and ask those folks how we can become Christians!"

9. "Don't worry, Billy. Those people are Christians—they must have a good reason why they're driving ninety miles per hour."

8. "What a joy to be sharing the highway with another car of Spirit-filled brothers and sisters."

7. "Isn't it wonderful how God blessed that Christian couple with a brand-new BMW?"

6. "Dad, how come people who drive like that don't get thrown in jail? Can we get a bumper sticker like that too?"

5. "Stay clear of those folks, Martha. If they get raptured, that car's gonna be all over the road."

4. "Oh, look! That Christian woman is getting a chance to share Jesus with a police officer."

3. "No, that's not garbage coming out of their windows, Bert—it's probably gospel tracts for the road workers."

2. "Oh, boy, we're in trouble now! We've just rear-ended one of God's cars!"

1. "Quick, Alice, honk the horn, or they won't know that we love Jesus!"

doing backstrokes in the belly of a blue fin—he had another job. He was an eighth-century prophet to the northern kingdom of Israel. God told him to go to Nineveh and preach to the city's Assyrian inhabitants—Israel's enemies who were cruel, vindictive, and idolatrous. God gave Jonah a message that would not likely make him any friends among the Ninevites: "Repent, for judgment is at hand."

Jonah liked that message of judgment. He wanted to call the forces of Heaven down to wipe out the evil of the Assyrians. But he gagged on the repentance message like a two-year-old on a two-dollar sucker. *How could God let them off the hook?* he wondered. *How could He give them a chance to repent?* Jonah was soon carrying a Jolly Green Giant-sized chip on his shoulder.

Jonah refused the assignment and ran away. He got a standby ticket aboard a cruise ship bound for Tarshish, a destination he thought was as far from Nineveh as a boat would take him. *"Jonah ran away from the LORD and headed for Tarshish. He went down to Joppa, where he found a ship bound for that port. After paying the fare, he went aboard and sailed for Tarshish to flee from the LORD"* (Jonah 1:3).

For a while the scenery was spectacular, but he soon discovered this wasn't one of those cruises featuring mini-concerts between bountiful breakfasts, luxurious lunches, dynamite dinners, and massive midnight snacks.

Jonah found out he was a passenger on the Good Ship Pepto-Bismol! Sometimes we, too, end up on the wrong boat. We sail along, admiring the beautiful sunrise and sunset, when all of a sudden the mast is broken, the sail is down, and we're bailing water! *"Then the LORD sent a great wind on the sea, and such a violent storm arose that the ship threatened to break up"* (v. 4).

Crisis has a way of creeping up on us. *"All the sailors were afraid and each cried out to his own god. And they threw the cargo into the sea to lighten the ship. But Jonah had gone below deck, where he lay down and fell into a deep sleep"* (v. 5).

THERE'S NO TIME FOR ANSWERS;
I'VE GOT TOO MANY QUESTIONS!"

Jonah didn't take a very long nap!

The winds and waves were tossing the ship like Tinkerbell in a typhoon! The crew and the other passengers weren't exactly throwing a reception in Jonah's honor:

> The captain went to him and said, *"How can you sleep? Get up and call on your god! Maybe he will take notice of us, and we will not perish."*
>
> Then the sailors said to each other, *"Come, let us cast lots to find out who is responsible for this calamity."* They cast lots and the lot fell on Jonah. So they asked him, *"Tell us, who is responsible for making all this trouble for us? What do you do? Where do you come from? What is your country? From what people are you?"*
>
> He answered, *"I am a Hebrew and I worship the LORD, the God of heaven, who made the sea and the land."*

vv. 6-9

179

Times of calamity are naturally times of intense questioning. We run through our checklist of possibilities:

"Why?"

"What?"

"Who?"

"How?"

Often we get so wrapped up in the questions that we don't have time to concentrate on the answers. But there always is an answer, God's answer.

> On a foggy night at sea, the ship's captain saw what appeared to be the lights of another ship heading toward him. He instructed his signalman to contact the other ship by signal light. He sent the message, "Change your course ten degrees to the north."
>
> The reply came, "Change *your* course ten degrees to the south."
>
> The captain responded, "I am the captain. Change *your* course ten degrees to the north."
>
> Response: "I am a seaman first class. You change *your* course ten degrees to the south."
>
> The captain was furious. He had his signalman reply, "I am a battleship. You change *your* course ten degrees to the north."
>
> Reply: "I am a lighthouse. You change *your* course ten degrees to the south!"[30]

That story wonderfully illustrates that it's not always clear what we are to do. And God's timing doesn't always fit with our time frame—God Standard Time isn't the same as People Standard Time. God has a loving purpose for every single event of our lives. *"'I know the plans I have for you,' declares the L*ORD*, 'plans to prosper you and not to harm you, plans to give you hope and a future'"* (Jeremiah 29:11).

Hope.

Future.

Two great promises are rolled into one: There's a way out, and there's a way through!

The "way out" often doesn't happen until later, but the "way through" is a present-tense promise.

FINDING ANSWERS IN AWFUL TIMES

A woman driving through Oregon over the Cascade Range ran into a snowstorm and became very frightened. She peered ahead and saw a snowplow. What luck! She kept as close to the machine as she could while it removed snow from the road. At times the heavy snowfall almost cut off her view, but her faithful guide kept on leading the way.

After some time, the plow stopped, and the driver got out and walked over to her car. "Lady, where are you going?" he asked.

I'm on my way to Central Oregon," she replied.

"Well, you'll never get there following me. I'm plowing this parking lot."

There is a reason for every season of life. As we've seen, God has a master plan for our lives, a plan that is absolutely beneficial to us, and we can trust that He is leading us on the right course. We only see the "rough" side of the answer, like viewing a tapestry from its underside. When searching for God's answers, it is important to keep the following principles in mind.

1. **Look for spiritual answers first.** The seasick seamen started looking for some answers to their dilemma at the right place—the spiritual aspect of the situation. They pulled Jonah from his bunk, sat him on a shaky chair on top deck, and began to grill him: *"They asked, 'What have you done?' (They knew he was running away from the LORD, because he had already told them so.)"* (Jonah 1:10).

Secular answers are never more important than spiritual ones. We were created for a right relationship with God, so the first place to check when things go awry is that relationship.

"How does my reaction to this traumatic situation reflect my relationship with the Lord?" If the answer is extreme *fear* instead of extreme *faith,* then we'd better take our spiritual auto in for an alignment!

2. **Be honest about my situation.** "Are there any personal attitudes or actions that have contributed to this calamity?"

Not every situation is self-inflicted, but some are. There are times when we simply suffer the consequences of our own behavior. As it says in Jonah, *"The sea was getting rougher and rougher. So they asked him, 'What should we do to you to make the sea calm down for us?' 'Pick me up and throw me into the sea,' he replied, 'and it will become calm. I know that it is my fault that this great storm has come upon you'"* (vv. 11-12).

Repentance is a major step toward healing. When we acknowledge sin in our lives and confess that sin, God brings healing in accordance with His promise. First John 1:7-9 says, *"If we walk in the light, as he is in the light, we have fellowship with one another, and the blood of Jesus, his Son, purifies us from all sin. If we claim to be without sin, we deceive ourselves and the truth is not in us. If we confess our sins, he is faithful and just and will forgive us our sins and purify us from all unrighteousness."*

3. **Refrain from trying to take charge.** When the situation seemed to be getting out of hand, the crew put their sailing experience into action. Instead of listening to Jonah's answer—the spiritual answer—they took matters into their own hands: *"Instead, the men did their best to row back to land. But they could not, for the sea grew even wilder than before"* (Jonah 1:13).

"Am I interfering with God's working by trying to solve this problem myself?"

As we see in the passage, when the sailors took matters into their own hands, it only got worse, *"The sea grew even wilder."* We've already discovered that the best way to handle a crisis is to relax and leave the driving to God.

4. **Some things are totally out of our control.** Two elderly women were out driving in a large car—both could barely see over the dashboard. As they were cruising along, they came to an intersection. The stoplight was red, but they just went on through. The woman in the passenger seat thought to herself, *I must be losing it. I could have sworn we just went through a red light.*

183

After a few more minutes, they came to another intersection, and the light was red again. Again, they went right through. The woman in the passenger seat was almost sure that the light had been red but was really concerned that she was losing it. She was getting nervous and decided to pay very close attention to the road and the next intersection.

At the next intersection, sure enough, the light was red, and they went on through. So she turned to the other woman and said, "Mildred, did you know that we just ran through three red lights in a row? You could have killed us both!"

Mildred turned to her and said, "Oh, am I driving?"

We are a remote-control generation. If things don't power-up, power-down, or change channels at our bidding, they're not worthy of our ownership. Jonah and the boys on the S.S. *Catastrophe* didn't have the power to change the channels. *"Then they cried to the LORD, 'O LORD, please do not let us die for taking this man's life. Do not hold us accountable for killing an innocent man, for you, O LORD, have done as you pleased'"* (Jonah 1:14).

"Am I willing to acknowledge God's ownership of this situation?" God's perfect will is like a mighty flowing river. We put up our little dams of doubt, or we try to dig little tributaries of tears and complaints. But the river keeps moving in all its spectacular power—like the mighty Niagara. The ways of the Almighty are perfect in their powerful purpose. He is a sovereign Lord, a God who will do *what* He pleases, *when* He pleases, and *how* He pleases, all for the loving benefit of the people He loves with an everlasting love. As soon as we are able to acknowledge that sovereign purpose, we are one step closer to the healing fountain.

5. **Trust God's timing.** *"Then they took Jonah and threw him overboard, and the raging sea grew calm"* (v. 15). For the sailors, the calm directly followed the calamity. It often does. No matter how the storm rages through the night, there is always a sunrise. Psalm 30:5 says, *"His anger lasts only a moment, but his favor lasts a lifetime; weeping may remain for a night, but rejoicing comes in the morning."*

God promises that there will be rejoicing—in His perfect time. As surely as the stars shine at night and the planets turn in their orbits, God will deliver on His promises. "Am I willing to wait for God's answers in His time?"

Each day comes bearing its gifts. Untie the ribbons.
—Pat Freeland

6. **Be careful about your vows.** Apart from taking up an offering, the sailors did the most spiritual thing they could think of: *"At this the men greatly feared the LORD, and they offered a sacrifice to the LORD and made vows to him"* (Jonah 1:16). World War veterans call this manner of making vows "foxhole promises." When the bombs were bursting overhead and the bullets were flying in their direction, soldiers were hunkered down in bunkers dug out of the earth called "foxholes." And when the scary times came, many of those soldiers made on-the-spot promises to God: "Lord, if You'll get me out of this situation, I'll. . . ." That spirituality was called foxhole faith because it lasted only as long as the crisis.

"Am I willing to keep my promises to God?" Searching for spiritual answers shouldn't be a temporary thing. It should extend beyond the calamities into our everyday lives.

> *Trust in the LORD with all your heart and lean not on your own understanding; in all your ways acknowledge him, and he will make your paths straight.*

Proverbs 3:5-6

7. **Answers aren't always obvious.** Job gave the right response regarding God's intervention during that dialogue with his buddies in the midst of the bad times. He said, *"He performs wonders that cannot be fathomed, miracles that cannot be counted"* (Job 9:10). The Bible says that God works in mysterious ways. His gifts of deliverance come in a wonderful variety—and they don't have the same wrapping.

"Am I willing to accept God's design for my deliverance?" Jonah had the most interesting side trip that any cruise-line passenger ever had! *"The LORD provided a great fish to swallow Jonah, and Jonah was inside the fish three days and three nights"* (Jonah 1:17). As I stated before, when we hear about Jonah, we usually associate him with a whale. "Great fish" is probably the best translation of the original Hebrew language. I don't think we ought to get lost in some theological cave here. I do know that we're usually suspicious of any story involving men and fish. Fish do tend to grow in size with each retelling of the fishing adventure story.

Could a whale or great fish actually swallow a man alive? Yes, if God orchestrated it! Focusing on the fish keeps us from the main point of the story, however. God used the belly of a fish as a meditation room where He could speak to Jonah's heart in quiet.

It wasn't the most obvious or the most ideal setting for a church service, but it worked! Very often, God doesn't use the most obvious—or the most ideal—settings to teach us the most important lessons. Frederick Buechner, one of my favorite writers, put it this way: "Jonah's relief at being delivered from the whale can hardly have been any greater than the whale's at being delivered from Jonah."

8. **God eventually will solve the problem.** Jonah had a spiritual revival in that sanctified submarine. He repented of his attitude. He asked God for a second chance. And he promised to do what he was supposed to do. Then God must have told the fish that if it didn't turn loose, he'd have this Hebrew bellyache all the way to his retirement party: *"The Lord commanded the fish, and it vomited Jonah onto dry land"* (Jonah 2:10).

"Am I willing to believe God for deliverance?" The best use of our spiritual energy in the midst of a crisis is to focus on the way out. All the answers don't come instantly in the awful times of our lives, but they will come if we simply put our trust in the Lord and wait for the sunshine.

Lord, if you're booking this cruise,
I've got my suitcase packed.

Once the core spiritual issues are settled, it's time to simply sit back and enjoy the cruise—as much as possible (knowing there will be times of turbulence and seasickness).

How do you trust the Lord in the turmoil? Here are a few simple suggestions:

1. **Trust God's Word.**

Devotional times during a dilemma? It may not seem reasonable, but it's the wisest thing to do. God's Word is terrific and timeless. There's a present promise for every situation. God instilled His perfect plan into the dedicated minds of His servants, who then used their equally dedicated hands to write it out. The Bible speaks for itself: *"Prophecy never had its origin in the will of man, but men spoke from God as they were carried along by the Holy Spirit"* (2 Peter 1:21).

Maybe you've heard the story of the Christian lady who had to do a lot of business travel. Flying made her nervous so she always took her Bible along with her to read, and it helped her to relax. On one flight she was reading her Bible while seated next to a businessman. When he saw her Bible, he snickered and went back to work on his laptop computer.

After a while, he stopped working, turned to his fellow passenger, and asked, "You don't really believe all that stuff in there, do you?"

The woman responded, "Of course I do. It's the Bible, God's Holy Word."

"Well, surely you don't believe all those stories!" he said. "What about that guy who was swallowed by the whale?"

She replied, "Oh, you mean Jonah? Yes, I believe that," the lady said as she held up her well-worn Bible. "I believe everything in this book."

He asked, "Well, how do you suppose he survived all that time inside the whale?"

"Well, I don't really know," the lady responded. "I guess when I get to Heaven, I'll just have to ask him."

"What if he isn't in Heaven?" the man asked sarcastically.

The lady replied quickly, "Then would you be so kind as to ask him for me?"

2. **Keep walking in obedient faith.**

John, another disciple of Christ, gave some Spirit-anointed advice about walking with the Lord through the daily rigors of life. He says, *"This is love: that we walk in obedience to his commands. As you have heard from the beginning, his command is that you walk in love"* (2 John 1:6).

God can't navigate you out of troubled waters until you give Him the helm. As you learn to obey His moment-by-moment commands, He guides you lovingly and carefully through your troubled times. Even the ability to live out the will of God comes from God Himself.

After Jonah's exit from the fish, he took a quick shower and started looking for his next assignment. *"Then the word of the LORD came to Jonah a second time: 'Go to the great city of Nineveh and proclaim to it the message I give you.' Jonah obeyed the word of the LORD and went to Nineveh"* (Jonah 3:1-3).

We can't say that Jonah was a quick study, but we can say that he was a good student! He learned to obey the Lord regardless of the consequences.

A faith that can't be tested can't be trusted!
—Warren W. Wiersbe

3. Be committed for the duration.

The apostle Peter wrote, *"Those who suffer according to God's will should commit themselves to their faithful Creator and continue to do good"* (1 Peter 4:19). Fainthearted faith won't hold you when the winds beat against your cruise ship. If you want to get through your storm, stick to God's promise like Teflon to a ten-inch frying pan!

You didn't commit to Christ just for the pencils on Friend Day or the potluck dinner on Homecoming Sunday! You committed to Christ because your past needed forgiveness and your future needed hope. Crisis times make good payback times—good times for telling Him how much you love Him. Problems are:

Predictors—They will mold our future.

Reminders—We are not self-sufficient. We need God and others to help us.

Opportunities—They pull us out of our ruts and cause us to think creatively.

Blessings—They open doors that we usually do not go through.

Lessons—Each new challenge will be our teacher.

Everywhere—No place or person is excluded from them.

Messages—They warn us about potential disaster.

Solvable—No problem is without a solution.[31]

190

4. Be willing to make adjustments.

If Jonah did any "Monday-morning quarterback" time, I'm sure he thought about how different his journey would have been had he just gone to Ninevah. If he had adjusted his attitude and his actions to the will of God, he wouldn't have taken that damp and dark detour!

God may call you to do or say things that don't look reasonable at first. But remember, you only see the trees; He sees the whole forest. Adjustments are for your safety and for your health—spiritually or otherwise.

5. Be patient and trust God's promises.

"He who pursues righteousness and love finds life, prosperity and honor" (Proverbs 21:21). That isn't some roll of the dice—it's the Word of God. As someone once said, both the steps, and the stops, of a good man are ordered by the Lord. If you let Him, He can work out His ultimate good, even in your worst dilemma.

The following story was told by Donner Atwood in *Leadership:*

During the terrible days of the Blitz, a father, holding his small son by the hand, ran from a building that had been struck by a bomb. In the front yard was a shell hole. Seeking shelter as quickly as possible, the father jumped into the hole and held up his arms for his son to follow.

Terrified, yet hearing his father's voice telling him to jump, the boy replied, "I can't see you!"

The father, looking up against the sky tinted red by the burning buildings, called to the silhouette of his son. "But I can see you. Jump!"

The boy jumped, because he trusted his father. The Christian faith enables us to face life or meet death, not because we can see, but with the certainty that we are seen; not that we know all the answers, but that we are known.[32]

6. Be obedient to God's will.

"Let the peace of Christ rule in your hearts, since as members of one body you were called to peace. And be thankful" (Colossians 3:15).

In an article in *Pulpit Digest*, John Townsend relates a story that illustrates the need for daily thankfulness.

One day, according to a time-honored story, Saint Francis of Assisi longed to see his brothers. They agreed to meet in a remote monastery in the Umbrian mountains of central Italy. After arriving and enjoying their reunion, each reported what he had experienced on the road.

One Franciscan brother who had traveled on muleback said: "God protected me in a miraculous way. When I was crossing a narrow bridge over a deep mountain gorge, the mule jumped. I fell and narrowly escaped falling over the wall of the bridge into the gorge. God by His love saved my life."

A second brother said: "I had to cross a river, and I slipped and fell. The waters carried me down the river. But God in His grace provided a tree which had fallen across the river. I could grasp a branch of that tree and pull myself ashore, thanks to God's miraculous mercy."

Then Saint Francis said: "Let us thank God for His wonderful works. I did experience the greatest miracle of all on my way. I had the smoothest, most pleasant, completely uneventful trip."[33]

Whether smooth sailing, or in the midst of a hurricane, there is room for thankfulness and a place of peace. If you're going through a "hurricane time," go to the place of peace. Get alone with God and let Him speak His peace to your troubled spirit. Tell Him you're committed for the duration. Let Him work His wonderful promises into your heart and mind.

Why did God go to so much trouble to hunt Jonah down, allow him to be tossed into the sea, and then force some fish to change to a Kosher diet? God had a thousand prophets as capable as Jonah. What's the point? Jonah needed spiritual surgery to straighten out the bitterness and prejudice of his heart. The hurt was allowed as God's way of teaching him.

It's often the same reason why we go through troubled times. The surgery experience is often fearful, frustrating, and painful, but healing comes after the surgery. God uses the pain for His purpose. It's His way of reaching us, loving us, teaching us, using us for His great cause. It's His way of revealing Himself to us.

Is there a great lesson in that life-threatening drama? Absolutely! The episode characterized the great drama that was to unfold later.

Jonah spent three days in the belly of a fish.

Jesus spent three days in a tomb—and then the Resurrection!

Resurrection comes after the rough times. We go through winds and waves on purpose. Those times are training times in which God can teach us His promises. They are also great times of bonding. God uses them to reveal His eternal love for us. In those times, we feel His arms around us in a very real way.

Buzzards may be circlin', but God will not fail us, not for one moment!

The Haven of Rest

My soul in sad exile was out on life's sea,
So burdened with sin and distress,
Till I heard a sweet voice saying, "Make Me your choice,"
And I entered the haven of rest.
I've anchored my soul in the haven of rest.
I'll sail the wide seas no more.
The tempest may sweep o'er the wild, stormy deep;
In Jesus I'm safe evermore.

—*Henry L. Gilmour, 1890*

The Undertaker May Be Smiling, but God's Not Finished with Me Yet

(Finding Hope above the Hardship)

I've often told people, jokingly, "The undertaker will be the last one to let you down!" The fact of the matter is, their business is dependent upon people dying.

There was a woman in the Bible who may well have been facing an unsolicited meeting with the undertaker. Shuffling along into the synagogue, she was likely a devout Hebrew woman. Perhaps the delight in her worship had long ago turned into duty. Her faith hadn't spared her the condition that had seemed to suck all of the hope from her life.

For eighteen years she had suffered under the burden of her infirmity. Probably it was a curvature of the spine that had twisted her gnarled frame. Bent over by the disease, she couldn't see the smiles on the faces of the passersby. She only heard their scorn.

It's all too likely that children laughed at her awkward appearance, that adults waiting in line behind her at the marketplace cursed her for her slow, methodical gait. In the Bible, Christ calls her a "daughter of Abraham." We may call her a daughter of despair. How many years had passed since she felt any twinge of promise? Every activity drove needlelike pains throughout her twisted body until she wore her discomfort like a heavy, woolen blanket.

Luke, the gospel writer who was also a physician, chronicles her condition:

> *On a Sabbath Jesus was teaching in one of the synagogues, and a woman was there who had been crippled by a spirit for eighteen years. She was bent over and could not straighten up at all.*
>
> Luke 13:10-11

Demonic power had dealt the crippling blow to her life. Agents of the one who came to "steal, kill, and destroy" had laughed with glee as they drew the gray curtain of depression over her countenance.

But they hadn't counted on Christ being at the temple that day! *"When Jesus saw her, he called her forward and said to her, 'Woman, you are set free from your infirmity'"* (v. 12). Her pain owned her like a slave master, but Jesus came along and set her free.

The touch of Jesus raised her—raised her above her infirmity, raised her above the great hardship of her condition. *"Then he put his hands on her, and immediately she straightened up and praised God"* (v. 13).

We need to look carefully at that sequence. The remedy for finding hope above the ruins is in the actions of the Master and in the reaction of the woman who was made whole.

I PUT MY DUCKS IN A TOMATO ROW,
SO NOW I HAVE QUACKERS IN MY SOUP.

The sequence of events that took place on that Sabbath day gives us insight into gaining spiritual victory over the things that cripple our spirits, souls, or bodies. We may have all of our "ducks in a row" medically, financially, emotionally, and socially but still miss the reason why that woman left the synagogue with a different attitude from the one she had when she'd arrived.

First, she came to the right source. She didn't find hope in any earthly institution.

Her family couldn't give it to her.

Her community couldn't give it to her.

Her religion couldn't give it to her.

What she couldn't do by her own efforts over the span of eighteen years, Jesus did in an instant. The Lord Jesus Christ is the only constant for turning despair into hope. The apostle Paul wrote a letter to Christians who lived in a place called Thessalonica. He greeted them with a reminder about their source of strength and victory saying, *"We continually remember before our God and Father your work produced by faith, your labor prompted by love, and your endurance inspired by hope in our Lord Jesus Christ"* (1 Thessalonians 1:3).

Throughout Scripture, things always got better when Jesus arrived:

The catering service for the wedding banquet at Cana improved noticeably after Jesus turned clear water into red wine (John 2).

When Jesus joined a funeral march for a widow's son, they lost a corpse and gained a marcher (Luke 7).

199

The disciples went fishing one night, cast their nets into the water, and pulled up *nets* until Jesus joined their group (Luke 5).

Jesus showed up at a barbecue where the demons of hell had planned to roast a father's son who was suffering from seizures. In a moment, hell lost its lunch, and the father gained a healthy son (Matthew 17).

Jesus visited a cemetery site, and His dearly departed friend Lazarus soon took a power walk (John 11).

When we go to Jesus as our source, it changes everything!

Second, she was in Jesus' line of sight. "Jesus saw her." When we go through buzzard-circlin' times, we often feel like nobody really cares about our condition. Think again! The tiniest sparrow can't even think about lunch without the Lord of the universe sending a memo to the chefs of Heaven to fix a worm casserole and deliver it to a tree branch. It says in the book of Matthew, *"Look at the birds of the air; they do not sow or reap or store away in barns, and yet your heavenly Father feeds them. Are you not much more valuable than they?"* (6:26).

He sees us—every tear, every frown, every sigh, every slumped shoulder, every furrowed brow. Our injuries are not insignificant to the Master.

He sees through the shadows.

He sees over the mountains.

He sees through the ceilings of the hospital.

He sees past the walls of the funeral home.

Walled prisons can't block His view.

Storm clouds can't block His view.

His all-seeing eye never blinks, even when we are sleeping. Jesus saw the woman, and His glimpse gave her hope.

Third, she listened for Jesus' voice. When Jesus called for her to come forward, nobody had to nudge her and tell her that He was speaking to her. She was already listening. The sounds of hope began to ring in her ears. Not only did the Master see her condition, but He was speaking to her need.

We begin to find hope above the hardship of life when we learn to listen for the Master's voice. But in order to hear His voice, we must focus, block out the other sounds, turn in His direction. Then we'll have to be ready to respond.

Fourth, she took Jesus at His word. He said she was "free from her infirmity." Without her step of faith—without making the effort to straighten up in obedience to His command—she would be hopeless still. Jesus told her she was healed. It was time to cast aside doubts like an unneeded crutch. Hope began for her when her faith reigned over the facts.

In another miraculous incident, a woman who had suffered from severe hemorrhaging interrupted Jesus on His way to perform a miracle in the life of a government official's daughter. Matthew 9:20-22 says: *"Just then a woman who had been subject to bleeding for twelve years came up behind him and touched the edge of his cloak. She said to herself, 'If I only touch his cloak, I will be healed.' Jesus turned and saw her. 'Take heart, daughter,' he said, 'your faith has healed you.' And the woman was healed from that moment."* Healed from what moment? *"That moment."* She was healed the moment she took the Lord Jesus Christ at His word.

Fifth, she moved forward in faith. Psychologist Karl Menninger said, "Hope is an adventure, a going forward—a confident search for a rewarding life." When Jesus touched the woman who had been bent over with His healing hands and when He pronounced her healing, the woman straightened up. Before that, the Scripture says, "she couldn't straighten up." What changed? Her attitude. The Master not only fixed her body, He also fixed her spirit. He gave her hope.

This woman had suffered too long. She was ready to try out her healing. For many years, she had shuffled along. Now she was ready to order a scooter from one of those upscale catalog companies! Hope begins when we move forward in faith. As long as we allow ourselves to be chained to our condition, we'll stay there. But when we take God at His Word, and when we take steps of faith, we'll discover a whole new world of wholeness.

Sixth, she didn't forget to praise the Lord. After she straightened her body up, her lips formed words of praise to her deliverer. Her soul rejoiced in the power of God. Hope is born in the sanctuary of our praise. The psalmist David expressed the song in his heart. Psalm 9:1-2: *"I will praise you, O LORD, with all my heart; I will tell of all your wonders. I will be glad and rejoice in you; I will sing praise to your name, O Most High."*

ORANGE CONES ON THE ROAD TO HOPE

If you spend much time traveling the interstate highways, you've probably encountered an orange cone or two.

I'm beginning to wonder if the orange cone business is actually the bedrock of our entire manufacturing industry. I wonder if there will be any orange cones in Heaven? I can envision the long line at the pearly gates, and somebody with a road sign and a walkie-talkie giving the saints directions through the cones.

I once heard a story about three guys who died at the same time and ended up in front of Saint Peter at the Pearly Gates. Saint Peter said to the first guy, "Why should I let you in?"

The guy answered, "I was a doctor, and I helped many people get well."

Saint Peter said, "Okay, you may come in."

Saint Peter asked the second guy, "Why should I let you in?"

The guy answered, "I was a lawyer and defended many innocent people."

Saint Peter said, "Okay, you may come in." Saint Peter then said to the last guy, "And why should I let you in?"

The guy answered, "Well, I was a managed-health-care professional, and I helped to keep health care costs down."

Saint Peter thought about it for a moment, then said, "Okay, you may come in, but you can only stay three days."

Fortunately, that's only a story. God doesn't run Heaven that way. The avenues of glory will be free from the obstacles we've encountered on earth—including orange cones. But our journey down here is a different story. Here, things aren't quite as clear. The apostle Paul intimated that we would get a little frost on our windshields now and then. He said, *"Now we see but a poor reflection as in a mirror; then we shall see face*

to face. Now I know in part; then I shall know fully, even as I am fully known" (1 Corinthians 13:12). And here on earth, some things are difficult to understand.

It wasn't long after the woman was healed that she encountered some orange cones. Her road to rejoicing—her brand-new hope—soon led to a detour sign. The chairman of the temple board had a hissy fit over the fact that Jesus had performed His work of healing on the Sabbath day; he put an orange cone in the road. *"Indignant because Jesus had healed on the Sabbath, the synagogue ruler said to the people, 'There are six days for work. So come and be healed on those days, not on the Sabbath'"* (Luke 13:14).

We shouldn't be surprised when we encounter an orange cone on Hope Road. Human nature has a way of working its way into our travels. Notice some of the orange cones we might expect:

1. TRADITION

The Jews were zealous in this matter of Sabbath-keeping, in accordance with the Mosaic Law. It was an important law, given to preserve the physical and spiritual energy of God's people. It said that one out of seven days in a week should be reserved for physical and emotional rest. The Sabbath also was to be observed by attendance to religious worship.

The religious leaders thought the law was not specific enough, so they set out to establish some *additional* traditions that would narrow what a person could or could not do on the Sabbath. They set some rigid restrictions. For example, their self-made law regarding work on the Sabbath limited the number of paces you could walk, the number of pounds you could lift, and the number of activities you could participate in.

Jesus didn't bypass the Law. In fact, He came to fulfill the Law. But He always butted heads with those who added to it—or at least those who were enslaved to it. The Master pointed to the orange cones:

> The Lord answered him, *"You hypocrites! Doesn't each of you on the Sabbath untie his ox or donkey from the stall and lead it out to give it water? Then should not this woman, a daughter of Abraham, whom Satan has kept bound for eighteen long years, be set free on the Sabbath day from what bound her?"*
>
> *When he said this, all his opponents were humiliated, but the people were delighted with all the wonderful things he was doing.*
>
> Luke 13:15-17

The Lord simply reminded the religious zealots that there is a more important work than crossing a *t* or dotting an *i*. And the bystanders on the healed woman's road of hope loved it! Our religious traditions may not give us a hope for the hardships of life, but that's not to say there isn't one! We may have to break out of the constraints of narrow-mindedness into the bold horizons of God's promises.

2. MISUNDERSTANDING

People may set an orange cone down on your Hope Road simply because they don't understand why you are so hopeful to begin with. Nonbelievers find it hard to understand why believers have smiles on their faces in a world like this. That's not a new phenomenon, however. Paul wrote to first-century Christians: *"The man without the Spirit does not accept the things that come from the Spirit of God, for they are foolishness to him, and he cannot understand them, because they are spiritually discerned"* (1 Corinthians 2:14).

During His earthly ministry, Jesus used illustrations to teach heavenly truths. These illustrations, called parables, were used to help people understand the principles of His kingdom. Jesus taught those who witnessed the woman's healing about the hope of this kingdom.

> *Then Jesus asked, "What is the kingdom of God like? What shall I compare it to? It is like a mustard seed, which a man took and planted in his garden. It grew and became a tree, and the birds of the air perched in its branches."*
>
> Luke 13:18-19

He countered their misunderstanding with some clear principles:

Principle one: The hope of God's kingdom begins small. *"It is like a mustard seed."* The tiny seed of this plant, common to the residents of Israel, actually grew into a tree that sometimes exceeded ten feet in height. But the emphasis was not on size; it was on power. The tiny seed of faith has power. It can grow to unbelievable size because of its inherent strength.

Size is deceptive, isn't it? Had I been on the salvation planning committee, I would have started bigger. In our soci-

206

ety, if big is good, bigger is better. If bigger is better, then biggest is best. I would have had Jesus come to earth as a conquering king. I would have had all the kings of the world march before Him and throw their crowns at His feet.

But that wasn't the way God chose to establish His kingdom. He began small: a helpless baby born in Bethlehem who was more like a tiny twig than a giant cedar. But He grew to be the Lord and Savior of the world: a giant sequoia. The King of kings. His kingdom grew to be greater than any other kingdom, and one day every earthly king will bow before Him!

Principle two: The hope of God's kingdom is realized by our participation. *"A man took and planted in his garden."* The gardener planted the seed personally. In the spiritual kingdom, there are some things we must do ourselves. God maintains the account, but we must write the checks. In another letter to the first-century church Paul wrote, *"My dear friends, as you have always obeyed—not only in my presence, but now much more in my absence—continue to work out your salvation with fear and trembling, for it is God who works in you to will and to act according to his good purpose"* (Philippians 2:12-13).

Principle three: The hope of God's kingdom grows with time. *"It grew and became a tree."* That hope was as tiny as a mustard seed at the beginning, but over time it grew. The best of God's kingdom is reserved for the last. Proverbs 4:18 says, *"The path of the righteous is like the first gleam of dawn, shining ever brighter till the full light of day."* Our hope may be very tiny at the outset of our trusting God, but as we continue to trust Him (even in bad times), it grows to completion.

Principle four: The hope of God's kingdom is to be shared with others. *"The birds of the air perched in its branches."* The wisdom and support that are ours now are to be shared with others later on.

> *Praise be to the God and Father of our Lord Jesus Christ, the Father of compassion and the God of all comfort, who comforts us in all our troubles, so that we can comfort those in any trouble with the comfort we ourselves have received from God. For just as the sufferings of Christ flow over into our lives, so also through Christ our comfort overflows.*
>
> 2 Corinthians 1:3-5

3. DISCOURAGEMENT

Discouragement suggests a lack of courage. It's a philosophy that the apostle Peter sought to counter when he referred to a people locked in time, who ignored the hope of Christ's return. *"They will say, 'Where is this "coming" he promised? Ever since our fathers died, everything goes on as it has since the beginning of creation'"* (2 Peter 3:4). To be locked in time is about as exciting as a macaroni-and-cheese buffet.

Years ago a hydroelectric dam was to be built across a valley in Maine. The people in the town were to be relocated, and the town was to be submerged.

During the interim time between making the final decision and actually evacuating the people, the town, which had once been a well-kept place, fell into disrepair. Because of the looming relocation, the townspeople saw no reason for maintaining their town. One of the city fathers rejected their philosophy and made an impassioned speech, saying, "Where there is no faith in the future, there is no work in the present."

Discouragement over the sameness of our situation can sap our very strength. Society says there is no way out, there is only an eventual destruction. It can only hope to soothe our imprisonment. The message of the kingdom is this: THERE IS A WAY OUT. In 1 Peter 1:3, it says, *"Praise be to the God and Father of our Lord Jesus Christ! In his great mercy he has given us new birth into a living hope through the resurrection of Jesus Christ from the dead."*

We have a *"living hope,"* for every day and for eternity.

> *When you're lonely, you wish for LOVE.*
> *When you're down, you wish for JOY.*
> *When you're troubled, you wish for PEACE.*
> *When things look empty, you wish for HOPE.*
> —*Anonymous*

SITTING IN THE BACK PEW DOESN'T MEAN
YOU'LL BE RAPTURED FIRST.

The whole back pew thing has always been a dilemma to me. I've often wondered if folks choose that pew, so they'll get a head start if the Lord should return during the worship service. Maybe they're locked in on that "last shall be first" Bible verse.

I've got some good news. The rapture isn't for any "reserved" section. Why, I believe there'll even be some folks on the platform who will be taken up! John, the disciple of Christ, looked out the window of time and caught a glimpse of eternity:

> *Dear friends, now we are children of God, and what we will be has not yet been made known. But we know that when he appears, we shall be like him, for we shall see him as he is. Everyone who has this hope in him purifies himself, just as he is pure.*
>
> 1 John 3:2-3

We're surrounded by the effects of sin:

hopelessness

moral decay

spiritual indifference

selfishness

division

anger

pleasure seeking

world conflicts

But there's sunshine behind those clouds. The Lord Jesus Christ has not only seen our condition, He has spoken the words to our hearts, just like He spoke to that woman who was crippled, "You are set free."

C.S. Lewis defined hope as a "continual looking forward to the eternal world." One day, and maybe soon, the kingdom of Heaven will come to earth. And the King of kings will reign forever and forever.

Three church board members sat and watched a telephone repairman working in front of the church. Within earshot of the repairman, they began to discuss the best positions for prayer.

"Kneeling is definitely best," claimed one.

"Not for me," another contended. "I get the best results standing with my hands outstretched to Heaven."

"You're both wrong," the third insisted. "The most effective prayer position is lying face down on the floor."

The repairman could contain himself no longer. He cupped his hands and shouted in their direction, "The best praying I ever did was hanging upside down from a telephone pole!"

Your whole world may be upside down right now—and in your spirit, you may be hanging upside down with it. It's not a time for hand-wringing, however. It's time to pray in faith. It's time to take French philosopher Victor Edman's advice, "Never doubt in the dark what God told you in the light."

Someone wrote,

We Will Never Know. . .

Joy . . . until we face sorrow.
Faith . . . until it is tested.
Peace . . . until faced with conflict.
Trust . . . until we are betrayed.
Love . . . until it is lost.
Hope . . . until confronted with doubts.

It's time to pack away those doubts like a 1970s leisure suit and put on the royal robe of righteousness. It's been freshly cleaned by the blood of the Lamb, pressed by the power of the Spirit in trying times, and paraded down the runways of time with great and mighty success.

The kingdom is here now. And the kingdom is coming as well. There may be a few buzzards circlin' overhead, but God hasn't failed you before—and He surely won't fail you now! There are 7,487 promises in God's Word with your name on them.

The undertaker may have sent word to his or her stock-broker and said, "I'll be sending a contribution to my IRA soon." But hold the phone!

God's not finished with you yet! Jesus Christ has already won your war. You don't have to look very far for a hope over the hardships of time. It's already yours—nonperishable, always fresh, unfading, and it even has your name on it. (See 1 Peter 1:4.)

Dr. Billy Graham once said, "Our confidence in the future is based firmly on the fact of what God has done for us in Christ. No matter what our situation may be, we need never despair because Christ is alive." Amen!

So grab that spiritual baseball bat and take a swing at those buzzards!

Endnotes

1 Stan Toler, *God Has Never Failed Me, but He's Sure Scared Me to Death a Few Times,* (Tulsa: RiverOak Publishers, 1998, 2001) p.43.

2 Ira F. Stanphill, "I Know Who Holds Tomorrow," (Copyright © 1950 Singspiration Music/ASCAP. Benson Music Group, Inc.)

3 Eugene H. Peterson, "The Jonah Syndrome," *Leadership Journal,* (Wheaton, Ill., CTI Publishing, 1990) p. 43.

4 Charles Swindoll, *Living Beyond the Daily Grind,* (Dallas: Word Publishers, 1988) p. 73.

5 Talmadge Johnson and Stan Toler, *Rediscovering the Sunday School,* (Kansas City: Beacon Hill Press, 2000) p. 47.

6 Paul Tournier, *The Adventure of Living,* (San Francisco: Harper and Row Publishers, 1965) pp. 125-127.

7 *USA Weekend,* "Fear: What Americans Are Afraid of Today." (August 22-24, 1997) p. 1.

8 Paul Tournier, *The Adventure of Living,* (San Francisco: Harper & Row, 1965) p. 123.

9 Arnold Lobel, *Frog and Toad Together,* adapted (San Francisco: Harper and Row, 1973) p. 8.

10 Jeannie E. Hussey, "Lead Me to Calvary," © 1921. Renewal 1949 by Hope Publishing Co., Carol Stream, Ill: 60188.

11 Tan, Paul Lee, *Encyclopedia of 15,000 Illustrations* (CD-Rom) /— NavPress Software 1998.

12 John Claypool, *Tracks of a Fellow Struggler,* (Dallas: Word Publ., 1976) pp. 38-39.

13 Bill Bright, *Discovering God,* (Orlando, Fla.: NewLife Publication, Campus Crusade for Christ, Inc. 1999).

14 Bonnie, Perry "After Dreams Die," *Moody Monthly,* (Chicago: Moody Press, July/August, 2000) p. 15.

15 "Servanthood, Works Righteousness," *Leadership* (Carol Stream, Ill.: Christianity Today, Winter 2000, Vol. 21 No. 1) p. 96.

16 Johnson, Derric, *Lists, the Book,* (Tulsa: Honor Books, 1995) p. 71.

[17] Jim Priest, "Family Talk," the *Daily Oklahoman*, Oklahoma City: July 21, 2000, p. 61.

[18] Charles L. Wallis, editor, *Speaker's Illustrations for Special Days*, (Grand Rapids: Baker Book House, 1956) p. 67.

[19] Stan Toler and Elmer Towns, *Year-Round Book of Sermon Helps*, (Ventura, Calif.: Regal Books, 2001) p. 306.

[20] Leith Anderson, "Valley of Death's Shadow," *Preaching Today*, Sermon Tape #131 (Wheaton, Ill.: CTI Publ.)

[21] Vance Havner, *Playing Marbles with Diamonds*, (Old Tappan, N.J.: Fleming H. Revell Co., 1968), pp. 94-95.

[22] Stan Toler and Debra White Smith, *The Harder I Laugh, the Deeper I Hurt*, (Kansas City: Beacon Hill Press, 2001) p. 86.

[23] *Christian Reader*, (January/February 2000), p. 79.

[24] Mother Teresa, *A Simple Path*, (New York, Ballantine Books) p. 114.

[25] Charles L. Allen, *Perfect Peace*, (Old Tappan, N.J.: Fleming H. Revell Co., 1979), pp. 137-138.

[26] *Houston Chronicle*, (Houston: Chronicle Publishers, 2/6/00) p. 20A.

[27] Stan Toler, *God Has Never Failed Me, but He Sure Has Scared Me to Death a Few Times!*, (Tulsa: RiverOak Publisher, 1998, 2001) p. 188.

[28] J. Ellsworth Kalas, *If Experience Is Such a Good Teacher*, (Nashville: Dimensions for Living, 1994.)

[29] *The Executive Speechwriter Newsletter* (Emerson Falls, St. Johnsbury, Vt.: Words, Ink, Volume 12, Number 2) p. 6.

[30] Rusty Wright, *500 Good Clean Jokes*, (Uhrichsville, Ohio: Barbour Publishing) p. 185.

[31] Dr. John Maxwell, *The Winning Attitude*, (San Bernardino, Calif.: Here's Life Publishers, 1984) p. 99.

[32] Donner Atwood, *Reformed Review*, Quoted in *Leadership* vol. 4, no. 4 (Carol Stream, Ill.: Christianity Today, Fall 1983), p. 87.

[33] John Townsend, *Pulpit Digest*, (Grove Heights, Minn.: Logos Productions, Inc., September/October 1979), p. 53.

About the Author

Stan Toler is senior pastor of Trinity Church of the Nazarene in Oklahoma City, Oklahoma, and hosts the television program "Leadership Today." For several years he taught seminars for INJOY Group—a leadership development institute. Toler has written over fifty books, including his best-sellers *God Has Never Failed Me, but He's Sure Scared Me to Death a Few Times; The Buzzards Are Circling, but God's Not Finished with Me Yet; The Five-Star Church;* his popular Minute Motivators series; and his latest book *The Secret Blend.*

To contact the author:

Stan Toler

PO Box 892170

Oklahoma City, OK 73189-2170

E-mail: stoler1107@aol.com

Web site: www.StanToler.com

Epilogue

Letters received from those who read

God Has Never Failed Me,
but He's Sure Scared Me to Death a Few Times

When my publisher, Mark Gilroy, asked me to include a few letters from my best-selling book, *God Has Never Failed Me, but He's Sure Scared Me to Death a Few Times,* I was ecstatic! I have received letters and e-mails from readers almost daily since the release of the book.

The letters are presented with great thankfulness to God for using the book to encourage people around the world.

Enjoy!

Thank you for an easy-to-read, down-to-earth book about the promises of God. Your book has reminded me of how crazy life can be. Whether we are experiencing small disappointments or a heart-twisting crisis, *God Has Never Failed Me, but He's Sure Scared Me to Death a Few Times* puts it all into perspective.

—Anne, *Pennsylvania*

Greetings from Singapore! I would like to say a big thank-you for your book *God Has Never Failed Me, but He's Sure Scared Me to Death a Few Times*. Frankly, I bought the book because of its cute cover and title. But, I need to tell you, your book with its funny stories and encouraging words has lifted me out of my depression. It's wonderful to know that God has a sense of humor.

—Mailyn, *Singapore*

Just a note to thank you for writing *God Has Never Failed Me, but He's Sure Scared Me to Death a Few Times*. It arrived in my home when problems were "stage center." I have bought twenty-five copies and given it out as gifts! Most importantly, my seventy-six-year-old dad read it and accepted Christ!

—Teresa, *Oklahoma City*

Just wanted to let you know I love your book *God Has Never Failed Me, but He's Sure Scared Me to Death a Few Times*. This book came to me at a crucial time in my life. I am thirty-nine and have developed a heart problem. Recently, I've spent several days in the hospital. Reading your book has helped me so much. I have read it more than once and bought several other copies for my friends. It has been an inspiration to me and has deepened my faith.

God bless you!

—Susan, *Vermont*

Greetings in Christ,

Just this morning I finished reading your book, *God Has Never Failed Me, but He's Sure Scared Me to Death a Few Times*. It came to me as a gift from a great friend, and I want you to know that it was EXACTLY what I needed at this point in my life. I am writing to you now, because I am a pastor in need of a pastor! I'm scared to death!

Humor—being on the alert for the absurdities of life and appreciating them with laughter—is a way of life for me, and I know God has a great sense of humor or He wouldn't have made me the way I am! Thank you for sharing your wonderful gift of humor and for blending it so well with faith and trust in God!

Blessings,

—Amy, *Tennessee*

I had about finished reading *God Has Never Failed Me, but He's Sure Scared Me to Death a Few Times* and had it laying upside down on my tray on the plane from Indianapolis to Denver. The stewardesses were in the aisle with their cart of drinks. All of the sudden one of them said to me, "That is really true, isn't it?" She was referring to the phrase on the back of your book, "God can do anything but fail!" I said, "It sure is." I said to her, "You really need to see the title of this book!" I showed it to her, and it really got her attention. We talked a little bit. She said she was in a Bible study in her church, etc. We talked just a little, and I all of a sudden said to her, "You give me your name and address, and I'll send you a copy of this book." She said she would, and she did.

Then she started telling the gal on the other end of the cart that she needed to see the book. She, too, was excited. She said she and this other gal had just been talking about God and whether He could do everything or not, etc., etc. Again I said to this lady, "Give me your name and address, and I'll send you a copy of this book." She, too, did. This morning I put in the mail the books and wrote them both a short little note.

This was a thrilling experience, and the words "God can do anything but fail!" is what got the one gal's attention. It is exciting to see what God does to touch people's hearts.

In Christian love,

—Stan, *Indiana*

I have just completed reading your book *God Has Never Failed Me, but He's Sure Scared Me to Death a Few Times.* Very inspirational! I'm a twenty-year-old freethinker who has been very cynical when it comes to religion. After reading your chapter on pinto beans and bologna, now that's a feast of faith, I have given my heart to Jesus Christ. Thanks!

—Jamie, *New York*

God has gifted you to speak to the heart with words of laughter and encouragement. As I read *God Has Never Failed Me, but He's Sure Scared Me to Death a Few Times,* there were times when I laughed and cried. Your stories reminded me of my childhood. It's a best-seller!

—James, *North Carolina*

Just a brief note . . .

I've been having a really tough time lately, perhaps the greatest spiritual crisis in my life. Tonight, your book *God Has Never Failed Me, but He's Sure Scared Me to Death a Few Times* touched me [in] a way that I cannot describe to you.

You will never know what you've meant to me tonight. Thanks,

—Roger, *Alaska*

The story about the Down's-syndrome child is very touching. It makes me realize that we can *all* work for God regardless of our limitations.

Thanks so much!

—Pat, *Wisconsin*

Enjoyed reading your book while traveling on a small plane in a rainstorm. The title of the book, *God Has Never Failed Me, but He's Sure Scared Me to Death a Few Times,* is super! Thanks for helping me find peace in the midst of a storm.

—Bob, *Ohio*

A day off, a hot cup of tea, and a good book—what could be better! I have thoroughly enjoyed reading *God Has Never Failed Me, but He's Sure Scared Me to Death a Few Times*. Your wonderful sense of humor, entertaining style, and uplifting words have made my day off special.

You are loved!

—Carol, *Florida*

With the recent loss of our son, your book *God Has Never Failed Me, but He's Sure Scared Me to Death a Few Times* is a breath of fresh air coming into our lives. God knows just what we need!

—Barney and Jenny, *Alabama*

Stan,

The book *God Has Never Failed Me, but He's Sure Scared Me to Death a Few Times*, has been such a blessing to me. The chapter, "Never Check Your Oil While Parked on a Hill," has especially ministered to me. I've been battling fear in several areas of my life. Your book has given me new courage!

—Debbie, *Illinois*

I appreciate your new book. It's true, *God Has Never Failed Me, but He's Sure Scared Me to Death a Few Times*, but there are times when I wonder why He created the Oklahoma Legislature!

Sincerely!

—Governor Frank Keating, *Oklahoma*